C000292608

Settle & Carlisle Revival

SETTLE & CARLISLE REVIVAL

THE LINE THAT REFUSED TO DIE

BRIAN SHARPE

First published in 2013 by Mortons Media Group

This edition published in 2021 by Gresley Books,
an imprint of Mortons Books Ltd.
Media Centre
Morton Way
Horncastle LN9 6JR
www.mortonsbooks.co.uk

Copyright © Gresley Books, 2021

All rights reserved. No part of this publication may be reproduced or transmitted in any form or by any means, electronic or mechanical including photocopying, recording, or any information storage retrieval system without prior permission in writing from the publisher.

ISBN 978-1-911658-54-2

The right of Brian Sharpe to be identified as the author of this work has been asserted in accordance with the Copyright, Designs and Patents Act 1988.

Typeset by Jayne Clements (jayne@hinoki.co.uk), Hinoki Design and Typesetting.
Printed and bound by Gutenberg Press, Malta.
10 9 8 7 6 5 4 3 2 1

Contents

Introduction

A 72-MILE RAILWAY running across the roof of England, reaching the highest point on any main line railway in the country, carrying not just a frequent and well-patronised passenger service popular with local inhabitants and tourists, but heavy long-distance freight traffic as well; we are probably lucky it was built at all... and even luckier that it has survived.

It is almost impossible to imagine a 72-mile abandoned trackbed passing through such places as Blea Moor, over Dent Head and Arten Gill viaducts and the legendary Ms Gill summit; worse still it could even be a long-distance footpath and cycleway now, with lots of informative signboards, none making any mention of the fact that it was once a railway line. We are lucky that sufficient people felt strongly enough to campaign successfully to stop this happening and keep one of Britain's favourite railway lines open.

The Settle & Carlisle line was built as part of a rather unnecessary third route from London to Scotland and probably would not have been built at all if an earlier scheme for a route via Ingleton had not failed.

It was a tough line to build through wild and inhospitable terrain, but once built the line prospered... and although by then a bit run-down, survived the Beeching axe in the 1960s. However, by the early 1980s, British Railways made a second attempt to close it and ran services down to a point where only the bare minimum passenger service was operating, with all but two of its stations closed.

Since then, not only was the line reprieved from closure again after an eight-year battle, but train services were expanded even while it was still the intention to close it, and that expansion has continued.

Saving the line was not the end of the story, it was just the beginning.

The timetabled services have increased in frequency, many closed stations have reopened and even heavy freight traffic has returned in significant quantity. Best of all, at least from many enthusiasts' perspective, is that steam-hauled excursions over the line have gone from strength to strength.

This book looks at the revival in the fortunes of the Settle & Carlisle, its regular passenger and freight traffic, diversions, excursions, its stations and infrastructure and especially the return of steam power.

CHAPTER 1

History of the Line

A COMPANY CALLED the North Western Railway announced plans in 1845 to build four sections of new railway line to connect the Leeds and Bradford Railway's extension at Skipton with the Lancaster and Carlisle Railway. Two of the lines planned by Charles Vignoles and Robert Stephenson were from Skipton to Lancaster, with a branch from Clapham through Ingleton to a junction on the West Coast Main Line near Low Gill, which would have created a shorter route from London to Scotland than either the east coast or west coast routes.

But before the necessary granting of royal assent in June 1846, two of the four proposed lines were abandoned and the branch to Low Gill was now going to be the main line. Work started on the construction at Ingleton within six months, but the construction work proved difficult and the engineers began to focus more on the other route, from Clapham to Lancaster. North of the terminus at Ingleton station, an 11 arch viaduct was necessary to cross the River Greta. The first train arrived from Skipton on July 30, 1849, but within a year the branch became one of the shortest-lived train services in railway history when the Ingleton section was abandoned as soon as the Lancaster line opened.

The missing link to Low Gill was eventually resurrected by the Lancaster and Carlisle Railway in 1858, and the L&CR, including the Ingleton branch, was leased to the London & North Western Railway. Meanwhile, the (Little) North Western Railway had been swallowed up by the Midland Railway, which now had a through route from London via Sheffield and Leeds to Ingleton, which reopened on September 16, 1861, but was not exactly the most appropriate northern terminus.

Relations between the MR and LNWR were bad. The LNWR would not give the MR running rights over its line north of Ingleton and the MR would not allow the LNWR to use its station in the town, so the LNWR opened its own at the northern end of the viaduct, and passengers had to change trains by walking about a mile over steep hills between the two stations.

By the 1860s, the main East and West Coast Main Lines served the key Anglo-Scottish market, but to compete for this traffic, the ambitious Midland Railway needed to secure an agreement for its goods and passengers to be carried by the LNWR from Ingleton to Carlisle and Scotland. It was possible since the routes were physically connected by the end-on junction at Ingleton.

BR's last steam train, 1T57, 'The Fifteen Guinea Special' climbs the 'Long Drag' near Horton in Ribblesdale on August 11, 1968, headed by BR Standard Britannia Pacific No. 70013 *Oliver Cromwell*. DAVE RODGERS

Forty years after the end of BR steam, LMS 8F 2-8-0 No. 48151 approaches Ais Gill summit with a southbound 'Dalesman' on July 27, 2008.

Class 47 No. 47552 departs passes Kirkby Stephen with a northbound 'Cumbrian Mountain Pullman' in April 1987, which will return steam-hauled from Carlisle. At this time, BR was still in the process of closing the line.

The Midland Railway started life as a regional railway based in Derby but was successfully expanding by acquisition of other railways and it was clear that it was going to monopolise the traffic between London, the East Midlands, South Yorkshire and on to West Yorkshire and beyond.

Eventually an agreement was reached, enabling the Midland to attach through carriages to LNWR trains at Ingleton, but the agreement was tenuous at the best of times and various sources recall such devious practices as Midland passengers having their coaches attached to slow-moving coal trains for the journey on to Carlisle.

Clearly the situation was unsatisfactory and by 1865, having considered a route via Settle and Hawes to connect with the East Coast Main Line, the MR had new plans for its own direct route to Carlisle via Appleby, and in June 1866, Parliamentary approval was given. Soon afterwards there was a financial crisis in the UK. Interest rates rose sharply, and the Midland's board, prompted by a shareholder revolt, reconsidered this risky and expensive venture where the estimated cost was £2.3 million (equivalent to £280 million in 2020).

As a result, in April 1869, with no work started, and with the LNWR now prepared to enter into a workable agreement, the company petitioned Parliament to abandon the scheme it had previously proposed. However Parliament, under pressure from other railways, including the Lancashire & Yorkshire and the North British, which would both benefit from the scheme that would cost them nothing, refused. The local population was particularly looking forward to the new main line being built and the MR was obliged to build the line after all and construction commenced in November that year.

The 11 arch sandstone viaduct 80ft over the River Greta spanning the divide between the MR and LNWR branches at Ingleton which carried the contentious route from Clapham to Low Gill and could have carried MR expresses to Scotland, avoiding the need for the Settle & Carlisle line to be built.

The line is engineered to follow the natural pathways through the hills of the Pennines, requiring 14 tunnels and over 20 viaducts. It was always seen as a main line trunk route so there was expected to be little local traffic, freight or passenger. The local people were perhaps not as well served as they might have been, with stations such as Dent being four miles away from and 600ft higher than the village it claimed to serve, and Kirkby Stephen station being 1½ miles away from the town. Construction of the Settle & Carlisle line began in 1869 and lasted for seven years with about 6000 men employed. It was the last main line railway in England to be constructed almost entirely by hand.

The navvies laboured in some of the worst weather conditions England can provide. Huge camps were established to house the navvies, many of them Irish. The MR helped pay for scripture readers to counteract the effect of drunken violence in an isolated neighbourhood. The camps were complete townships including post offices and schools and at Ribblehead had names such as Inkerman, Sebastopol and Jericho.

The remains of one of these camps – Batty Green – where more than 2000 navvies lived and worked, can be seen near Ribblehead. A plaque in the church at nearby Chapel-le-Dale records the workers who died – both from disease and accidents – building the railway. The engineer for the project was John Crossley, a Leicestershire man who was a veteran of other major MR schemes.

The terrain traversed is some of the bleakest and wildest in England, and construction was halted for months at a time due to frozen ground, snowdrifts and flooding of the works.

By 2012 the fortunes of Kirkby Stephen station had been revived. The major change in evidence is the installation of a footbridge for the first time in the station's history.

The plaque at Ribblehead recording the names of the shanty towns during construction.

Railway Openings in the Yorkshire Dales

- 1849 Skipton-Ingleton (North Western Railway) opened.
- 1850 Clapham-Lancaster (NWR) opened,Clapham – Ingleton closed.
- 1861 Ingleton-Low Gill (Lancaster & Carlisle) opened, Clapham – Ingleton reopened.
- 1867 Wennington-Carnforth (Furness & Midland Joint) opened.
- 1875 Settle Junction-Carlisle opened to goods traffic.
- 1876 Settle Junction-Carlisle opened to passenger traffic.

The line was engineered to express standards throughout. It reaches a height of 1169ft at Ais Gill summit and to keep the gradients down to no steeper than 1-in-100, which is necessary for fast running using steam traction, huge engineering works were required. Even then, it was impossible to avoid a 16-mile climb from Settle to Blea Moor, almost all of it at 1-in-100, which became known to enginemen as 'the long drag'.

The line opened for freight traffic in August 1875 with the first passenger trains starting on May 1, 1876. There were three standard designs for all station buildings on the line, known as Small, Medium (or Intermediate) and Large, but built in differing local materials. Although it had not wanted to build the line, the MR dominated the market for London-Glasgow traffic, providing more daytime trains than its rival, the LNWR. In 1923 The MR was merged, along with the LNWR, into the London Midland & Scottish Railway. In the new company though, the disadvantages of the MR route were clear: its steeper gradients and greater length meant it could not compete on speed from London to Glasgow. The MR had competed on the extra comfort it provided for its passengers but this advantage was lost in the new company. The LMS put all its resources into the WCML, and by comparison, the S&C became somewhat neglected.

After Nationalisation in 1948, the pace of rundown quickened. It was regarded as a duplicate line, and control over the through London-Glasgow route was split over several regions which made it hard to plan popular through services. Mining subsidence affected speeds through the East Midlands and Yorkshire. In 1962, the 'Thames-Clyde Express' travelling from St Pancras via the S&C took almost nine hours from London to Glasgow, against a fastest time of seven hours 20 minutes over the WCML.

CHAPTER 2

The Big Society

THE SETTLE & Carlisle line survived Dr Beeching's 1963 plan for reshaping the railways but all the intermediate stations except Settle and Appleby were closed from May 4, 1970. In 1981, BR made it known that it intended to close the line to passengers completely and just retain short sections to serve industrial sites. The main issue was stated to be the cost of repairing and waterproofing Batty Moss viaduct at Ribblehead as it was in such poor condition. A manager, Ron Cotton, was appointed by BR with the specific task of managing the closure of the line.

In 1984, the Government and BR gave formal notice that it was intended to close the line in view of the heavy financial losses. The fight against the closure was the largest campaign of its kind ever seen in this country, with more than 26,000 written objections. Every legal loophole or minor error in the closure notices was exploited so the process dragged on for five years. 'Closure' manager Cotton attracted many passengers to use the line, and local stations were reopened in 1986 following a series of walkers' charter trains operated under the DalesRail banner from 1975 with local authority support.

While the case for closure remained largely based on the condition of Ribblehead viaduct, an experimental repair on one arch to assess the total cost showed that this would actually be much lower than anticipated. In 1988 the Government announced it was "minded to close the line" but would give three months breathing space to see if a proposal could be found to operate the line privately.

No such viable proposal was received. However, in April 1989 the minister for transport announced that the closure was cancelled due to the great public interest in the line, the improvement in the number of passengers using it and the lower than anticipated cost of repairing Ribblehead viaduct. In making this decision, the minister, Michael Portillo, hoped that the vast public pressure which had been mounted to save the line could now be turned into a positive means of improving its fortunes.

But this was not the end of the story; rather, it was just the beginning. In granting the line's reprieve the minister suggested the formation of a charitable trust to assist with future restoration of buildings and structures along the line. What has happened has been a remarkable success story of partnership between public and private bodies which has seen the S&C transformed into a healthy and vibrant railway with a positive future outlook. Three organisations together form the Settle-Carlisle Partnership.

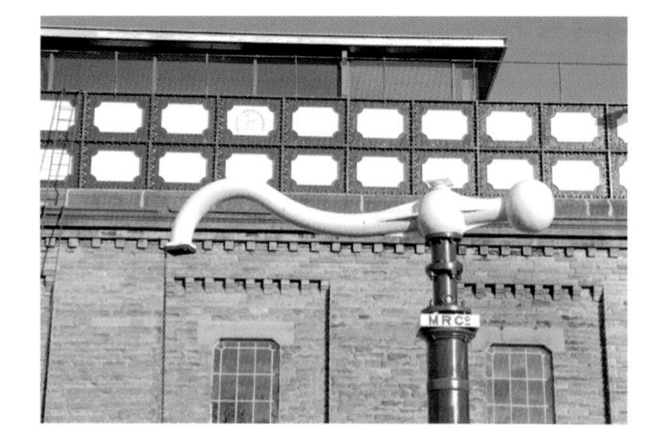

The Settle-Carlisle Railway Development Company was formed in 1992 as a limited by guarantee, not for profit partnership to encourage sustainable commercial development. Senior figures in the region formed the company to provide a powerful network to stimulate appropriate development involving all the local authorities and public sector bodies in the region surrounding the railway.

The company moved from strength to strength and now handles the promotion of both the Settle-Carlisle line and the route between Leeds, Lancaster and Morecambe. Projects include the production of the full colour line guide/timetable twice a year, funding the guided walks programme and leaflet and the operation of the Dales railcard scheme.

The projects team has been instrumental in funding major infrastructure projects including waiting shelters, a footbridge at Kirkby Stephen, heritage lighting at Settle station, and a refreshment trolley service on some services on the line.

The Settle and Carlisle Railway Trust is a registered charitable trust formed in 1990 to help preserve, restore and maintain historic buildings and structures along the line and to promote public knowledge and appreciation of the line.

The eight trustees, currently under the chairmanship of Bryan Gray, are drawn from those who have considerable experience in railways, civil engineering, law, accountancy and senior business management. The trust works to maintain a close relationship with the Friends of the Settle-Carlisle Line, The Settle-Carlisle Railway Development Company, Network Rail and Northern, the Train Operating Company.

The trust was involved in four major projects which were completed in the 1990s. Firstly the repairs to Ribblehead viaduct for which the revised estimate was between £2.75m and £3.25m. Repairs started in 1989 and were completed in 1993 at a cost of £3m. The shortfall in the BR budget was made up by generous grant funding from English Heritage, Railway Heritage Trust, Rural Development Commission and The Settle and Carlisle Railway Trust.

Secondly was the reinstatement of the northbound platform at Ribblehead station which had been demolished in the 1970s to make way for a new siding serving the quarry.

Thirdly, major refurbishment work was carried out on the station buildings at Hellifield, with the removal of later inappropriate additions. Fourthly a footbridge, originally from Guiseley and surplus as part of the Leeds north west electrification project, was installed at Kirkby Stephen. It was to a standard Midland Railway pattern, and after refurbishment was erected in 1998, providing much improved access for passengers to the northbound platform. Installation was carried out by Railtrack.

The trust's first major solo project was the restoration of the station building at Ribblehead. Most of

the structure required major work to bring it back into use. It acquired the building on a 125-year lease in September 1999 and completely refurbished it, converting it into a visitor centre housing a display tracing the history and development of the line in the Ribblehead area. It opened in June 2000.

The trust turned its attention to Horton in Ribblesdale. Again, Railtrack had done some restoration work in 1997, but much would be required to make it habitable. In August 2002 the trust completed the acquisition of the building on the same basis as Ribblehead and refurbished and converted it for office use, including the high quality restoration of original features. The office was successfully let. Next came Kirkby Stephen, again structurally repaired by Railtrack in 1998. This one was much larger, being a Type 1 'Large' design, but it offered more scope for improved accommodation and alternative uses. It was again converted for office use and successfully let.

At the other end of the scale, the station clocks on the S&C were not maintained and most disappeared after 1967, only Appleby retaining its clock in working order. When the trust started work at Kirkby Stephen, the remains of the clock were restored and inspired the restoration of clocks to other stations. A fundraising appeal raised £10,000 for clocks at Horton, Ribblehead, Dent, Langwathby and Lazonby – high-quality reproductions but electric rather than clockwork.

A major project in 2012 was the stationmaster's house at Ribblehead which became redundant in 1967 when the station became an unstaffed halt, being sold for use as a private house and changing hands again in 1985. After acquiring the station, the trust took an interest in the stationmaster's house. Renovation work costing around £300,000 was completed in 2013 and the house has since been marketed as a holiday home sleeping up to four people.

The Friends of the Settle Carlisle Line was originally formed in 1981 to campaign against the proposal to close the route. Since 1989 when the line was reprieved, it has acted as a user group to improve facilities and services for passengers. Eight stations have been reopened, the number of trains has increased, station buildings have been refurbished, platforms raised and Victorian style lamps installed. To complement the activities of Network Rail, the Train Operating Company, the Development Company and the Trust, the Friends has restored the disused signalboxes at Armathwaite and Settle station.

It operates a station adoption scheme where members tend the flower beds and look after the station welfare. It also helps to produce and distribute promotional leaflets to boost passenger numbers, and organises guided walks from some trains. The Friends' aims are to see all the stations fully restored; Anglo-Scottish trains running again and regular services on the line from Lancashire.

CHAPTER 3

Timetabled services

THE ORIGINAL timetable for the Settle & Carlisle line was four express and three stopping passenger trains daily (not Sundays), which increased in the line's heyday to nine express (including four overnight sleeping car services) and six stopping trains, reducing by 1960 to a similar level to 1880. The premier trains on the route in its heyday were through trains from St Pancras to Glasgow, 'The Thames-Clyde Express' and to Edinburgh, 'The Thames-Forth Express'. The former acquired its name in 1927, running north of Carlisle over the GSW route.

Both lost their names during the Second World War, but BR reinstated the former in 1949, while the latter remained unnamed until 1957, when it was reborn as 'The Waverley', running north of Carlisle over the NBR's route of that name through Sir Walter Scott country to Edinburgh's Waverley station. They were not fast trains and used a variety of former Midland Railway routes at various times, the Glasgow train taking up to 10 hours 30 minutes for the journey while the Edinburgh train in early BR days took up to 11 hours 17 minutes in the Up direction.

'The Waverley' became a summertime only train and ceased running on closure of its namesake route north of Carlisle in January 1969, while the 'Thames-Clyde' lost its name in 1974, although the train continued to run but via the WCML north of Carlisle. In 1975 the service was truncated to run only from Nottingham to Glasgow, and from 1982 diverted away from the S&C to run via Manchester.

Even in the mid-1960s, the line's stopping trains serving the local stations comprised three or four coaches departing from the bay platform at Hellifield behind anything from an LMS Ivatt 2-6-2T to a Clan Pacific.

The 1963 Beeching Report into the restructuring of British Railways recommended the withdrawal of all passenger services from the line, many smaller stations having closed in the 1950s. The Beeching recommendations were shelved, but in May 1970 all stations except for Settle and Appleby West were closed, and the line's local passenger service was cut to two trains a day in each direction.

Although the original Beeching withdrawal of passenger services did not happen, a further proposal was for total closure as a through route with just a single track branch from Settle Junction to Horton in Ribblesdale and from Carlisle to Kirkby Stephen for freight only. Again this did not happen.

Closure notices were posted on the remaining

Closed in 1970, but reopened in 1986, Ribblehead station had its Down platform reinstated in 1993.

The Class 45 and 46 Peak diesels were associated with the line for many years, and remained in use on the Nottingham to Glasgow expresses in the 1970s. A Peak crosses Batty Moss viaduct at Ribblehead on April 21, 1984.

A Northern Rail Carlisle to Leeds service passes Ais Gill on January 28, 2012.

Local stopping trains were in the hands of first-generation Diesel Multiple Units in the 1980s, but at least one set was restored to something approaching original BR green livery. A four-car DMU passes Settle Junction on May 16, 1987.

Class 31 No. 31412 heads uphill past Selside cottages on August 25, 1990.

stations three times between 1983 and 1984, but this seems to have prompted a huge increase in passenger numbers, from 93,000 in 1983 to 450,000 by 1989. Some of this was no doubt due to the appointment of Ron Cotton, supposedly to manage the closure process, but who not only expanded the train service but is now quoted as saying he actually disagreed with the closure plans and even found a loophole which permitted the reopening of eight of the closed stations on the line, with local authority help.

Of course, BR was not going to invest in new trains for a line it intended to close and this perhaps added to the line's enthusiast appeal. First-generation DMUs on the infrequent stopping trains and locomotive-hauled stock in the hands of already-ancient Class 31 and 47 diesels on the slightly-faster 'expresses' were kept in service until 1990, after which Class 156 Sprinter units finally appeared, replaced by Class 158s after 2007. Since 1989, considerable work has been done along the line in upgrading stations and facilities.

After privatisation, services on the line were operated by Arriva Trains Northern, a Train Operating Company which suffered several problems, including shortages of drivers and rolling stock and a prolonged period of industrial action.

The franchise covering much of northern England was eventually split with S&C services transferring to Northern Rail on December 12, 2004. Arriva Rail North took up the franchise on April 1, 2016, but was beset by industrial action, worsening punctuality and claims of poor customer service. The franchise period ended early – on March 1, 2020 – and since then the franchise has been run directly by the Department for Transport under the brand name Northern Trains.

CHAPTER 4

Freight Traffic

IN STEAM days, the S&C was an important freight artery and carried much of the wagon-load goods traffic typical of the era. Freight traffic originated on the route, from the gypsum mines of the Eden Valley and the limestone quarries on the Settle-Blea Moor section.

Although spared by Beeching in the 1960s, BR still wished to be rid of the line, but at the same time continuation of the WCML electrification from Crewe to Carlisle and Glasgow reinforced the S&C's value as a diversionary route. It appeared to have been spared though when the WCML electrification was completed in 1974, with track and signalling upgraded on the basis of only continuously-braked freight trains being allowed to operate. There were still a lot of unfitted or partially fitted freight trains and these became concentrated on the S&C.

But although this prolonged the life of the S&C, it was only until BR could rid itself of unbraked freight trains, which did not take too long as wagonload freight traffic was already in terminal decline.

Wagonload freight traffic all but disappeared from the rail network in the 1970s and by the 1980s freight traffic over the S&C was non-existent, the gypsum mines were largely closed and the quarries sent their produce by road.

By 1982, with two passenger trains a day each way and minimal freight traffic, and with phenomenally expensive viaducts to maintain, it really did look as if the line's days were numbered. The last regular freight traffic ceased in 1983, a year after the through passenger trains.

Although the gypsum traffic had dried up, the works remain at Newbiggin, and this has seen a role reversal in that gypsum now flows to the works, from power stations, largely as a result of tightened emissions regulations. The first train arrived in 1994 spearheading the revival of S&C freight traffic, and opening the way for coal trains to become commonplace for the first time in the line's history.

Coal, the lifeblood of many freight arteries, was never a major source of traffic for the line; there was simply no point in moving coal from England to Scotland or vice versa, both countries had plenty and it would have almost literally been a case of taking coal to Newcastle.

The virtual cessation of deep mining in Britain though led to major changes in the transport of coal, which is still required in vast quantities by power stations.

Domestic and even other industrial use of coal is now almost non-existent. Traditional coalfields

Colas Rail Class 66 No. 66849 *Wylam Dilly* brings the Friday only log train out of the loading sidings at Ribblehead. It will go to Blea Moor loop, reverse and head for Chirk on the Welsh borders.

Class 66 No. 66111 heads the evening Clitheroe-Mossend (Glasgow) cement train past Ribblehead. FRED KERR

A Freightliner Heavy Haul Class 66 works a Hunterston-Cottam power station coal train over Dent Head viaduct on August 8, 2012.

A Class 60 crosses Batty Moss viaduct with the daily empty gypsum train from Kirkby Thore running at that time to Drax power station.

have been wiped out. Most coal is destined for power station use but comes from much further away than used to be the case, often imported, and there are now a number of long-distance regular block trains of coal. Several originate from Scotland, either opencast coalmines or the sea terminal at Hunterston.

With coal being destined for the power stations of the Aire Valley in Yorkshire, Rugeley in Staffordshire or Fiddler's Ferry near Warrington, the Settle & Carlisle line has been able to play a major role, taking the pressure off the East Coast and West Coast routes. Hunterston was opened in 1979, originally for imported iron ore for the steelworks at Ravenscraig, but since closure of the steelworks, coal is the main import. In recent years, however, there has been a decline in coal traffic.

Another traffic flow is timber – mainly from Scotland to Chirk on the Welsh borders, but in 2012 there was even a weekly train carrying logs from Ribblehead, the train being loaded in the sidings which formerly served the nearby quarry. Additional signals were installed at Horton-in-Ribblesdale and other locations at a cost of £18 million to increase line capacity.

CHAPTER 5

Return to Steam

THE SETTLE & Carlisle was certainly not BR's last steam main line. The Southern Region Waterloo to Salisbury and Bournemouth/Weymouth line retained regular steam hauled expresses right up to electrification in July 1967. Although both routes north to Carlisle, the West Coast Main Line over Shap and the Settle & Carlisle over Ais Gill, saw steam workings up to the end of 1967, these were mostly on freight trains, albeit often in the hands of Britannia Pacifics.

However, steam-hauled expresses could still be seen in 1967 if only on summer Saturdays when two northbound relief trains over the S&C were rostered for Holbeck based Jubilees, becoming therefore the last pre-nationalisation express engines to haul express trains. This lasted until the end of September that year when the North Eastern Region became fully dieselised and steam workings over the S&C were then very much reduced.

Once the Carlisle area was dieselised at the end of December 1967, steam virtually disappeared from the line although there was still the occasional working from Carnforth through Settle Junction, up until the end of BR steam on August 4, 1968, which was marked by several steam railtours, some covering the Settle Junction-Carnforth line but none venturing north over the S&C.

The line did have its moment of glory a week later though when BR's very last steam train ran from Liverpool and Manchester via Blackburn to Carlisle and back. '1T57' or the 'Fifteen Guinea Special' was headed north to Carlisle by BR Standard Pacific No. 70013 *Oliver Cromwell*, and returned south behind LMS 'Black Five' 4-6-0s No. 44781 and No. 44871, after which the Britannia ran south light engine bringing the steam era to a close in the country which invented it. Before then, a couple of privately preserved main line steam engines had hauled railtours over the S&C, but in October 1967, BR had introduced a ban on such locomotives on its tracks, so this particular era was extremely shortlived.

After what to many people seemed a lifetime, the BR steam ban was lifted with effect from the summer of 1972, but with steam heavily restricted to just a few routes, the Settle & Carlisle not being one of them.

The 'approved' routes though did quickly expand and steam would almost certainly have returned to the 'Long Drag', if it were not for the fact that the WCML to Glasgow had been electrified in 1974, and it was not felt that steam engines could be allowed into Carlisle station. Just one very small exception was made on the occasion of the centenary of open-

The engine which had brought steam back to the Settle & Carlisle 12 years earlier: Under a stormy sky, LNER V2 2-6-2 No. 4771 *Green Arrow* runs non-stop through Hellifield with a southbound 'Cumbrian Mountain Express' on September 22, 1990. At this time the standard format for the 'CME' was to work from Leeds to Carlisle and return using two different engines. The stock was normally Pullman again by this time, supplemented by chocolate and cream Mk.Is.

BR Standard 4MT 2-6-0 No. 76079 and LMS 'Black Five' 4-6-0 No. 45407 approach Hellifield from the Blackburn line with Kingfisher Railtours 'Dalesman' from Manchester Victoria on March 25, 2005.

LMS Princess Royal Pacific No. 6201 *Princess Elizabeth* departs from Hellifield northbound on July 25, 1987, with a tour from Euston marking the 150th anniversary of the opening of the London terminus. The use of a full train of maroon Mk1 stock was unusual at this time.

ing of the S&C in May 1976, when two light engines were allowed to steam the two miles or so from Settle Junction to Settle station. Naturally it poured with rain all day.

However, steam engines are not incompatible with overhead 25kv electrification, after all Crewe station was electrified in the early 1960s and saw steam until 1967. Eventually, after some tentative experiments elsewhere, it was agreed that steam could run into Carlisle station under very tight guidelines and the way was clear for a steam train over the Settle & Carlisle line once again.

The day was Easter Saturday, March 25, 1978, and this time it snowed. The engine was LNER V2 2-6-2 No. 4771 *Green Arrow* from the National Railway Museum at York, which returned south two days later on Easter Monday in better conditions, both runs being very leisurely with long stops at various stations.

They were deservedly popular and several more trains ran during 1978, two trains on the same day on September 30, featured no less than three engines; No. 4472 *Flying Scotsman*, No. 35028 *Clan Line* and No. 92220 *Evening Star*. But this did not last long either. One reason for the S&C's survival is that it is a useful diversionary route, and in early 1979, Penmanshiel tunnel on the ECML between Berwick and Edinburgh, collapsed. It would take all year to reopen the line and as a result the S&C saw so many extra trains that there was no room for steam throughout 1979.

Then in 1980 came the 'Cumbrian Mountain Express'; this was a regular steam working almost every other Saturday, operated by SLOA Marketing, the railtour arm of the Steam Locomotive Operators Association which co-ordinated all main line steam running. A large part of the appeal of this train was that although it ran from Euston, tickets were valid from any BR station using connecting services. The train ran either clockwise or anti-clockwise from Carnforth, one steam engine working Carnforth-Hellifield, a second engine Hellifield to Carlisle or vice versa.

But even this much more significant return to steam was already under more serious threat. Having now re-established itself in a big way, the

HELLIFIELD

ALTHOUGH THE Settle & Carlisle Railway is generally regarded as starting from Settle Junction and running for 72 miles north to Carlisle, passengers on the line see little of Settle Junction and usually not much of Settle itself. For many long-distance travellers, the journey over the Settle & Carlisle starts at Hellifield.

Unlike Settle Junction or Settle, Hellifield was a major railway centre with extensive sidings and a locomotive shed. It may be a shadow of its former self but it remains one of the Midland Railway's most impressive surviving stations in the north of England, the convergence of routes from Yorkshire and Lancashire and a place where steam trains either pause for water, change engines or reverse direction.

From a low point in the 1980s when even the signalbox was rarely open and the buildings were derelict, the station has recovered some of its former glories and facilities have been much improved – but the set-up remains far from ideal. Water columns have been installed so that steam engines can take water more easily but it is still almost always necessary for this to happen with the train in the goods loop so that service trains can overtake, and consequently passengers cannot board or alight.

Hellifield is a Midland Railway station but the line from Blackburn was part of the Lancashire & Yorkshire Railway. The village's original station opened in 1849, was south of the present site but was replaced by the present one in 1880 when the L&Y route opened. Stopping passenger services from Blackburn ceased in 1962 but as long as the S&C survived, so too did the route down the Ribble Valley. It formed part of the WCML diversionary route and although daily timetabled trains may be long gone, passenger trains have continued since 1975 under the DalesRail banner.

The cement works at Clitheroe has been a reliable source of traffic, sometimes flowing south and sometimes north, and although the line speed is 45mph, at least it is still double track throughout. Regular passenger services have again run from Blackburn as far as Clitheroe since 1987 although this does severely restrict the paths available for other trains on the line, but it is hoped that timetabled services will run through to Hellifield and beyond in the not-too-distant future.

future of steam, and the very future of the line itself, was threatened by BR's desire to close it completely.

Steam operations were largely organised around the location of suitable engines and it was fortunate that Carnforth shed had become Britain's biggest centre for main line steam, fairly conveniently located for S&C steam operations. The involvement of the Hon. William McAlpine who had become the owner of world-famous LNER A3 Pacific No. 4472 *Flying Scotsman*, based at Carnforth from the mid-1970s to the mid-1980s, certainly helped.

In 1985 though, steam returned to London on a regular basis. Steam over the Settle & Carlisle line is deservedly popular, but its popularity and that of other northern routes was perhaps artificially enhanced for many years by BR's reluctance to allow steam on routes in London and the Home Counties.

Eventually, a subtle change of policy saw *Flying Scotsman* and others move south to run particularly from Marylebone and on Southern Region routes. This in turn led to the slow decline of Steamtown at Carnforth, and although it remained as a locomo-

LMS Princess Royal Pacific No. 46203 *Princess Margaret Rose* approaches Hellifield after taking water at Long Preston on March 19, 1994.

LMS Jubilee 4-6-0 No.5690 *Leander* is on a Keighley to Settle Junction shuttle working at Hellifield.

Hellifield is often used to change from diesel to steam power. Class 46 Peak No. 46014 arrives at the then derelict station from Newcastle on March 20, 1983, from where LNER K1 2-6-0 No. 2005 will take the train to Middlesborough via Carlisle. The stock is Metropolitan-Cammell Pullman cars restored to original livery.

tive servicing base, it closed as a public museum. The 'CME' continued on a more or less regular basis, with the format changing, sometimes only using one engine, at other times using two but running Leeds-Carlisle and return with steam. SLOA Railtours was variously known as Pullman-Rail, Flying Scotsman Services, and later Past-Time Rail, set up by Bernard Staite who had played such a prominent part in the return of steam to BR main lines.

British Railways was privatised in 1994 and its Inter-City Special Trains Unit, which ran nearly all main line steam trains, was bought by Pete Waterman's Waterman Railways, based at Crewe. There might have been little change except that David Smith set up a railtour company which threatened the monopoly which Waterman thought he enjoyed. Privatisation put a stop to BR's arbitrary rules about where and when steam trains could run, and when David Smith's West Coast Railways chose Carnforth as its base, and became a Train Operating Company, with the right to run steam anywhere over the Railtrack system, it could only be good news for Settle & Carlisle steam.

In fact, a slight hiccup was that steam over Shap suddenly became commonplace for the first time in nearly 30 years, but if anything this benefited the S&C with trains able to cover both routes in a day.

Waterman Railways as a Train Operating Company was shortlived and the grand plan saw steam operations come under the umbrella of English Welsh & Scottish Railways (EWS), a freight haulage company, but with national coverage unlike any of the new passenger TOCs. EWS, of American origin, was acquired by German railway company DB Schenker, which seldom runs steam trains over the S&C today. However, West Coast Railways, with the S&C on its doorstep, regularly runs steam operations on the line during the summer months with its Carnforth-based engines, many of authentic LMS pedigree, playing a prominent part.

CHAPTER 6

Settle Junction

SETTLE JUNCTION is where the Settle & Carlisle line really begins. Originally it was not a junction at all but on the North Western Railway's route from Skipton to Ingleton, later Lancaster. In 1875 though, the S&C opened – first just to freight traffic; this was a double track express main line to Scotland and the Lancaster line was quickly relegated to branch status.

Settle Junction is the bottom of a pronounced dip. Northbound trains would run downhill from the summit near Otterburn, through Hellifield and Long Preston, rattling across the junction as fast as possible as after a few yards of level track it was here that they hit the bottom of the 1-in-100 gradient which continues for 15 miles to Blea Moor.

There was once a station at Settle Junction but little trace remains today, although the station house survived in private ownership until demolition in the late 1960s. Settle Junction signalbox is a typical Midland Railway 'box of timber construction dating from 1913 and is of course still operational. It houses a London Midland Region standard frame of 31 levers and controls the junction and the block sections south to Hellifield, north Blea Moor to the north and west to Carnforth Station Junction, currently the longest block section on the UK rail network at just over 24 miles which severely restricts the capacity of the Carnforth line. The junction itself was rebuilt from the traditional double track layout on both routes to the simplified ladder junction following a derailment in 1979.

Settle Junction signalbox.

LMS Jubilee 4-6-0 No. 45593 *Kolhapur* was a regular engine on the Settle & Carlisle line in the summer of 1967, the last summer of the Jubilees and the last year of BR steam on the line. It was preserved by Pat Whitehouse on withdrawal at the end of September 1967 and has been based at Tyseley in Birmingham, but it only ever returned to the northern fells for a couple of railtours in 1987. No. 5593 in LMS maroon livery passes Settle Junction with a SLOA 'Cumbrian Mountain Express' which it worked from Leeds to Carlisle on March 21, 1987.

A Railfreight-liveried Class 47 approaches Settle Junction with a diverted Up West Coast Main Line express on March 11, 1989.

LNER A4 Pacific No. 4498 *Sir Nigel Gresley* comes off the Carnforth line and passes the junction with an empty stock train from Carnforth on June 9, 1984, which will form the Clitheroe Parish Council 'Clitheronian' tour to York.

The SLOA 'Cumbrian Mountain Express' of July 29, 1981, carried a 'Wedding Belle' headboard in recognition of the wedding of the Prince of Wales and Lady Diana Spencer on that day. The train was headed from Carlisle to Skipton by SR 4-6-0 No. 850 *Lord Nelson*, seen coasting downgrade towards Settle Junction.

CHAPTER 7

Settle

HAVING JUST hit the bottom of the 1-in-100 climb to Blea Moor, most passenger trains are then obliged to stop at Settle just a couple of miles further on. The gradient eases to 1-in-200 but only for the station itself. Until the early 1960s, most expresses stopped at Hellifield but not Settle, and this only changed after BR was persuaded by the Settle stationmaster, named Taylor, to stop trains at Settle rather than Hellifield.

In West Yorkshire, and with a population of around 2500, Settle is thought to have seventh century origins, its name, originally spelt Setel, being the Angle word for settlement, but the area was described in the Domesday Book as "waste". However, a market charter was granted by Henry III in 1249 and a market square developed. The main route through the medieval town was on an east-west direction towards Giggleswick, the first bridge over the river Ribble being mentioned in 1498. Among the town's claims to fame, Ye Olde Naked Man is believed to be the oldest cafe in the country.

Immediately overlooking the town is Castlebergh, a 300ft limestone crag, containing several caves, one being Victoria Cave, so called because the inner chamber was discovered on the day of Queen Victoria's accession. It contained remains of mammoth,

A Freightliner Class 66 heads coal empties north past Settle on August 8, 2012.

Settle signalbox, closed in 1984, is open to visitors on Saturdays.

The renovated Midland Railway water tower.

The footbridge, installed in 1993, came from Drem on the East Coast Mail Line.

A Leeds-Carlisle train pauses at Settle.

Passengers waiting for the 11.04am to Leeds are treated to the sight of LNER A4 Pacific No. 60009 *Union of South Africa* passing with a Railway Touring Company 'Cumbrian Mountain Express' from Crewe to Carlisle on August 4, 2012.

bear, reindeer, hippopotamus and flint, a harpoon head carved from antler and other items.

The turnpike, Keighley to Kendal road, now the A66 trunk route, was constructed in 1753 and in the late 18th century cotton spiralling became the town's main employment. The North Western Railway reached Giggleswick, originally known as Settle Old in 1847, and in 1849 the railway company constructed Station Road from Giggleswick to Settle. But in 1876 the Settle & Carlisle line was opened and Settle then had a station in the centre of town. The station included a goods shed, sidings, cattle dock, signalbox and water tank, much of which survives today and has been renovated. Goods facilities though were withdrawn by BR in 1970. Interestingly, the footbridge is not original, Appleby being the only S&C station to be provided with a footbridge in Midland Railway days. The present one was installed in 1993.

Settle Mickey (and Minnie)

ABOVE THE platform at Settle station can be seen Mickey Mouse, but few travellers will be aware of how Mickey came to be there. Legend has it that in the big freeze of 1963, when trains were stuck in snowdrifts that were as high as telegraph poles, a gang was sent out to clear the line and found Mickey on top of one of the telegraph poles. He was rescued and put on display at Settle. How his better half Minnie also came to be there as well is not recorded.

Seen from the hillside above the town, LNER A4 Pacific No. 60009 *Union of South Africa* passes Settle with a Railway Touring Company 'Cumbrian Mountain Express' from Crewe to Carlisle on August 18, 2012.

A northbound service from Leeds arrives at Settle, passing the restored signalbox.

CHAPTER 8

Settle-Horton

CLIMBING AWAY from Settle, on a high embankment on a steady 1-in-100 gradient, the train has barely left Settle before it is passing the village of Langcliffe. The Craven Lime Company's Langcliffe quarry and the adjacent Hoffmann lime kiln, started operations in 1873 and had a rail-connected siding which was in use even before the line was fully opened to Carlisle, but it closed in 1931 and the kiln is now a preserved ancient monument.

Beyond Langcliffe, it is no distance to the next village of Stainforth, in the Yorkshire Dales National Park under Stainforth Scar, which was given its name by the Anglo-Saxons and written down in the Domesday Book as Stainforde. This means 'stony ford' which referred to the ford by the stepping stones across Stainforth Beck. It was a farming community and belonged to Sawley Abbey near Clitheroe.

In the 18th and 19th centuries, Stainforth had two water-powered cotton mills, a linen works, leather and paper making, and brewing. Stainforth became a parish in its own right with the consecration of St Peter's Church in 1842.

A bypass was built in 1974 to take traffic away from the centre of the village and prevent lorries grounding on the bridge over Stainforth beck. North of Stainforth, the line passes through the short Taitlands tunnel, taking it under the B6479 Settle to Ribblehead road. Taitlands is an early Victorian house built for Thomas Redmayne and his family from 1831. From 1942 to 2007 Taitlands was a Youth Hostel, but was then renovated to become a venue for weddings and events. In 2020, the property went on sale for £1.8m.

From Settle, the River Ribble is to the west of the railway but there are two viaducts at Sheriff Brow 300 yards apart. The southerly one is named Sheriff Brow Viaduct and the more northerly of the two is named Little Viaduct or alternatively Ribble Viaduct. The line crosses the Ribble twice in quick succession with the river then remaining to the west of the line on to just beyond Helwith Bridge.

Helwith Bridge is a tiny settlement alongside the railway, but it does boast the Helwith Bridge Inn. It is overlooked by the giant Arcow limestone quarry, although it is now many years since the quarry sent any of its products out by rail. Just north of the village, the railway one again crosses the River Ribble which then remains to the east of the line to Ribblehead.

Running an hour late LNER A3 Pacific No. 4472 *Flying Scotsman* climbs away from Settle past Langcliffe, returning from York to Carlisle on July 4, 1987.

LMS Princess Coronation Pacific No. 46233 *Duchess of Sutherland* is northbound at Langcliffe with a Railway Touring Company 'Cumbrian Mountain Express' from Crewe to Carlisle on August 21, 2012. DAVE RODGERS

The Hoffmann Kiln

A Class 45 Peak heads a Glasgow-Nottingham train past Langcliffe in April 1987, with the then virtually complete Hoffmann kiln clearly visible.

THE HOFFMANN kiln is the most common kiln used in production of bricks and some other ceramic products. It was patented by a German called Friedrich Hoffmann originally for brickmaking in 1858, but it was later used for lime-burning. The fire may burn continuously for years, even decades. In Iran, there are kilns that have been working continuously for 35 years. Any fuel can be used and the kiln can be any size.

In the British Isles there are only a few Hoffmann kilns remaining, the only ones with a chimneys being at Prestongrange Industrial Heritage Museum in Scotland and Llanymynech in Wales. The Hoffmann kiln at Langcliffe was built in 1873 and had 22 individual burning chambers. Limestone was brought from the quarry in the cliff face by a narrow gauge horse tramway running through a tunnel under a huge spoil heap. It was burned continuously in a circuit around the kiln and it took an average of six weeks for one whole circuit.

Limestone came from the quarry face in the cliff to the east under a huge spoil heap by means of a narrow gauge horse tramway running through a tunnel. Behind the burning zone, there were two or three chambers where lime was left to cool down before being loaded on to wagons in the sidings. The kiln is lined with firebricks and a limestone rubble core, which helped to keep the heat in.

Crushed coal was dropped down small chutes in the roof to keep the limestone burning. Air was drawn through the flue holes in the side under the burning limestone and the smoke went up the centre of the kiln to the chimney. In full production, the kiln employed 90 people. The quarry and kiln closed down in 1931, although the kiln was fired up one more time in 1937. In 1951, it was intended to ceremoniously demolish the chimney, but it collapsed anyway the day before with no one there to witness it.

LMS Jubilee 4-6-0 No.45596 *Bahamas* approaches Sheriff Brow with a northbound 'Cumbrian Mountain Express' on August 10, 1989.

A sight which disappeared from BR almost overnight was the parcels train, Class 47 No. 47503 heads such a train away from Stainforth and approaches Sheriff Brow on September 23, 1990.

BR Standard 8P Pacific No. 71000 *Duke of Gloucester* is on its first run over the Settle & Carlisle, crossing the viaduct at Sheriff Brow on September 23, 1990.The first coach is a GWR dynamometer car.

The pioneer English Electric Type 4 diesel D200 was returned to service in green livery for special duties but also formed regular power for one return working over the S&C for several years, D200 runs downhill at Helwith Bridge on June 20, 1987.

Helwith Bridge.

LMS Jubilee 4-6-0 No.45596 *Bahamas* struggles with damp rails at Helwith Bridge on October 19, 1991. This was a tour to Carlisle which had unusually originated at Oxenhope on the Keighley & Worth Valley Railway where the unique double chimneyed Jubilee is based. The train is in fact barely moving at this point and the locomotive stalled several times on the climb. Such problems led to a steam ban being introduced by BR during the autumn 'leaf fall' season.

CHAPTER 9

Horton-Ribblehead

AT HORTON-IN-RIBBLESDALE station, the line has reached a height of 850ft. Horton-in-Ribblesdale became a parish town in the early 12th century when the church of St Oswald was established. In the 13th century the village and parish were ruled by rival monastic orders at Jervaulx Abbey and Fountains Abbey. Not until 1315 was this dispute firmly settled, when Edward II confirmed the Abbot of Jervaulx as Lord of Horton-in-Ribblesdale.

In 1597, like so much of northern England, the village was struck by a killer plague, as confirmed by the parish burial register, which lists 74 deaths that year, roughly one-eighth of the parish population.

The region is popular for caving and potholing, with Alum Pot and the Long Churn cave system just to the north of the village, and Hull Pot and Hunt Pot on the western side of Penyghent. Horton in Ribblesdale is the traditional starting point for the Three Peaks walk, while both the Pennine Way and Ribble Way long-distance footpaths pass through part of the village.

The Three Peaks walk is an endurance challenge of 26 miles, including 5000ft of ascent and descent of the mountains of Penyghent, Whernside and Ingleborough which all has to be completed in under 12 hours and attracts thousands of walkers each year. The walk is usually (but not always) done in an anticlockwise direction starting/finishing in Horton-in-Ribblesdale.

The Horton-in-Ribblesdale welcome sign dates from the Millennium.

The circuit is also used for a fell race in April, while the Three Peaks cyclo-cross race also visits the three summits in the course of a longer 23.6 miles route on the last Sunday in September. Participants in both the running and cycling race regularly achieve winning times of around three hours, and sometimes both races are won by the same competitor. Horton station is the 'Small' type of station building to be found on the Settle & Carlisle line. In the 1950s, it was looked after by a station-

One of the most unusual steam workings over the S&C in recent years was the movement of NBR J36 0-6-0 No.673 *Maude* with two Caledonian Railway coaches from the Scottish Railway Preservation Society's Falkirk base to the Liverpool & Manchester Railway 150th anniversary celebrations on Merseyside in 1980. The short train coasts downhill through Horton-in-Ribblesdale on May 17, 1980.

LMS Royal Scot 4-6-0s were associated with the S&C for many years and No. 46115 *Scots Guardsman* worked a last Royal Scot-hauled railtour over the line on February 13, 1965. But it was August 2008 before a Scot once again did battle with the Long Drag, and again it was No. 46115, which had been preserved on withdrawal. The Scot passes Horton-in-Ribblesdale with West Coast Railways' 'Settle-Carlisle Venturer' on August 16, 2008.

A Class 47 heads a diverted West Coast Main Line express through Horton-in-Ribblesdale on March 11, 1989.

master called Taylor, who won the Best Kept Station award for 17 consecutive years, before moving on to take charge of Settle station. Horton lost its passenger service in 1970 along with all the other smaller stations on the route.

The station was reopened in July 1986, and has been refurbished by the Settle and Carlisle Railway Trust after some restoration work by Railtrack in 1997. In August 2002 the trust completed the acquisition of the building, carried out the necessary work to make it habitable and refurbished and converted it for office use, including the high quality restoration of original features.

The office was successfully let and the building is once again one of the most attractive on the line with beautifully kept gardens maintained by a volunteer gardener. The signalbox just to the south of the station, remained open until 1984.

Selside is a tiny village next to the railway just north of Horton, and dominated by the peak of Penyghent. Its signalbox was a relatively late survivor and on closure in 1975 was relocated to the Steamtown Railway Museum at Carnforth.

Pen-y-ghent is one of the Yorkshire Three Peaks, 2277ft (694m) high. The origins of the name of the peak are obscure.

In the Cumbric language Pen originally meant 'hill' or 'head', but ghent could be taken to be 'edge' or 'border'.

The name Penyghent could therefore be taken to mean 'hill on the border'.

Alternatively, it could also mean 'wind' or 'winds' – from the closest Welsh language translation as gwynt. So it might mean simply 'head of the winds'.

Drivers of northbound vehicles cannot fail to know they are passing through Selside.

Milages were originally from Settle Junction, but altered in 1914 to read from St Pancras.

The altitude and distance sign is a recent recreation of that of stationmaster Taylor.

LMS Princess Royal Pacific No. 6201 *Princess Elizabeth* heads up the 'Long Drag' past Selside on July 20, 1991.

DBS Class 66 No. 66137 heads the Fiddler's Ferry to Newbiggin gypsum train on August 2, 2012.

LNER A3 Pacific No. 4472 *Flying Scotsman* heads past Selside on July 4, 1987.

CHAPTER 10

Ribblehead

RIBBLEHEAD, AS its name suggests, is the source of the River Ribble. The B6479 road from Settle meets the B6255 Ingleton to Hawes road just here so it was natural that there would be a settlement. However, the nearest settlement before the coming of the railway was further west, at Chapel-le-Dale. Ribblehead station was effectively built to serve the hamlet and a few isolated farming communities, and was briefly named Batty Green.

The population expanded significantly when the railway was being built but once open there was little reason for anyone to stay. However, when the large Salt Lake limestone quarry was established west of the station towards Ingleborough, a few cottages were built close to the station and a Station Inn was opened next to the bridge taking the railway over the road to Ingleton.

The station was originally named Batty Green, but renamed Ribblehead from 1877 and it was a station with a difference; the stationmaster was trained in meteorological matters and his duties included the collection of rain and wind speed data for the Meteorological Office in London and although the stationmaster did not conduct them personally, Sunday church services were held in the station building until 1956.

The station was closed between 1970 and 1986 but is now leased by the Settle and Carlisle Railway Trust which has completely restored and refur-

Chapel-le-Dale church.

No. 37405 arrives at Ribblehead on February 20, 2004, during the period when Arriva Trains was using top & tail EWS Class 37s on one return train a day due to a shortage of multiple units.

LMS Princess Coronation Pacific No. 46229 *Duchess of Hamilton* departs from Ribblehead with a southbound 'Cumbrian Mountain Express' on August 25, 1990.

A cairn to commemorate completion of the repairs was unveiled by Roger Freeman MP, Minister of State for public transport on June 15, 1992.

bished it. There are resident caretakers, a small shop selling memorabilia, and its visitor centre includes exhibits about the history of the line and the fight to keep it open. An interesting exhibit is the original station sign.

From August 2005 the visitor centre has also housed a small exhibition about the Midland Railway Company which built the line. This is an outreach collection provided by the Roy F. Burrows Midland Collection Trust whose main exhibition is to be found in the Derby Industrial Museum.

Overlooking Ribblehead is the 2372ft (723m) peak of Ingleborough. On its western side is a large limestone plateau appropriately known as White Scars, below which are the White Scar Caves, the entrance series of which has been developed as a show cave. The plateau is bounded by Ravenscar, the longest plateau is bounded by Ravenscar, the longest unbroken cliff in the district, and on top of it is the pothole of Meregill Hole. The plateau to the north of Norber, an area known as The Allotment, is particularly rich in potholes; one of these, Long Kin East, is relatively easily accessible for 100 yards. Also located here is Juniper Gulf, which descends 420ft (130m) underground.

Ribblehead or Batty Moss viaduct is 440 yards long, and 104ft above the valley floor at its highest point. It is made up of 24 arches of 45ft span, with foundations 15ft deep. The north end of the viaduct is I3ft higher in elevation than the south end. It was designed by the engineer John Sydney Crossley. The first stone was laid on October 12, 1870 and the last in 1874. One thousand navvies building the viaduct established shanty towns on the moors for themselves and their families, named the towns after victories of the Crimean War, sarcastically for posh districts of London, and Biblical names.

There were smallpox epidemics and deaths from industrial accidents; meaning that the church graveyard at Chapel-le-Dale had to be extended. One hundred navvies were killed during the construction of the viaduct.

In 1964, several brand new cars being carried on a freight train that was crossing the viaduct were blown off the wagons carrying them and landed on the ground by the viaduct. A large part of the threat to the survival of the Settle & Carlisle line in the 1980s was the £6 million estimate for repairs to the viaduct. Several alternative schemes were put forward but eventually BR went ahead with the viaduct repairs. A noticeable change is that in the meantime the track was singled and now runs along the centre of the viaduct, which avoids the possibility of two heavy freight trains crossing the viaduct simultaneously.

Class 20s No. 20061 and No. 20093 approach Ribblehead station with a BR special on November 25, 1989. Class 47 No. 47444 is providing electric train heating.

2008-built LNER A1 Pacific No. 60163 *Tornado* steams past Ribblehead station on October 3, 2009.

LMS Princess Coronation Pacific No. 46229 *Duchess of Hamilton* performs a photographic runpast over Batty Moss viaduct for train passengers on a southbound 'Cumbrian Mountain Express' on June 9, 1984.

A two-car DMU crosses the viaduct northbound on July 25, 1987 before reversing at Blea Moor to form the first train of the day from Ribblehead to Leeds.

CHAPTER 11

Blea Moor

HAVING CROSSED the viaduct, the track becomes double again as it approaches Blea Moor, curving sharply to the east. At Blea Moor is a signalbox, passing loops and the remains of a number of sidings. There is little else other than the signalman's cottage alongside the 'box, a familiar sight but unfortunately not in the ownership of Network Rail or the S&C Trust.

The signalbox is to a standard LMS design and was built in 1941 to replace the MR 'box on the opposite side of the line when the Down sidings were extended.

According to the Ordnance Survey map, Ribblehead the place is in fact a little way to the east along the road to Hawes, although the river continues even further, it does not flow under the viaduct or anywhere near it. No water course actually flows under the viaduct, the nearest is the River Doe which rises a little towards the west but flows towards Ingleton. However, Force Gill flows over the line on an aqueduct close to Blea Moor tunnel and Little Dale Beck actually flows over the tunnel. Blea Moor is an isolated spot which even the signalman has a long walk to, although it is well-served by footpaths and passed by many walkers on the ascent to the 2415ft summit of Whernside, a long shapeless fell to the north-west, but which is the highest point in the ceremonial county of North Yorkshire, its summit lying on the county border with Cumbria. Whernside is easily confused with the lower peaks of Great Whernside and Little Whernside, both several miles to the east. The word 'Whern' is believed to refer to querns (millstones) while 'side' is derived from the Norse 'Saettr', meaning an area of summer pasture.

Ingleborough dominates the view of Blea Moor looking south. The summit is a broad plateau half a mile wide covered in dry turf, its distinctive appearance being due to the unusual geology of the underlying rock. The base of the mountain is composed of ancient Silurian and Ordovician rocks with a 600ft thick layer of carboniferous limestone above it. The many streams flowing down are soaked up by the limestone and fall into potholes. Above are the layered Yoredale series of sedimentary rocks, mainly shale and sandstone, and mostly concealed by the peat but revealed in the escarpments about 1700ft. There are layers of harder limestone between the softer rocks which have been eroded faster, but which protect softer rocks below them.

The very top is a cap of millstone grit, all softer rock above it having been completely eroded away, creating a flat summit. Where the path from Ingle-

The pioneer Class 40 diesel D200 approaches Blea Moor with a Leeds-Carlisle train on August 18, 1983.

Running two hours late, LMS Princess Royal Pacific No. 46203 *Princess Margaret Rose* passes Blea Moor signalbox with a northbound railtour on January 2, 1995.

Blea Moor signalbox.

ton reaches the summit rim is a large cairn which is the remains of a battlemented round tower, built in 1830 to be used as a hospice. It was never used as its opening ceremony became so drunken that parts of it were destroyed there and then, and the rest not long later.

Along the northern and eastern edges is the shattered wall of a military camp, believed to be Roman, but perhaps originally Celtic. The fort was used by the Romans all year round, Britain's climate being much milder in Roman times.

The 2629 yard (2404m) Blea Moor Tunnel is the longest tunnel on the Settle-Carlisle Line, being almost twice as long as the second longest at Rise Hill. It took more than four years to complete, passes some 500ft below the moor after which it was named and was built with the aid of seven separate construction shafts sunk from the moor above. This permitted no fewer than 16 separate gangs of workers to be used during construction (one from each open end and two from the foot of each of the shafts). Four of these shafts were subsequently filled in but three were retained for ventilation purposes and are still used today.

From Blea Moor sidings, trains enter a deep cutting and pass beneath the Force Gill aqueduct just before entering the tunnel.

Soon after entering the tunnel, trains have topped the mostly 1-in-100 'long drag' from Settle Junction and start to run downhill at 1-in-440 through the tunnel, although the actual summit will not be reached until after a further but easier climb from Garsdale to Ais Gill.

BP Standard 8P Pacific No. 71000 *Duke of Gloucester* emerges from the southern portal of Blea Moor tunnel on July 1, 1991. JOHN SHUTTLEWORTH

After emerging from the tunnel and passing Blea Moor signalbox, Class 31 No 31428 *North Yorkshire Moors Railway* is about to enter the single track section across the viaduct with a southbound train on May 26, 1990.

Seen from the east side, LNER A2 Pacific No. 60532 *Blue Peter* passes Blea Moor with a NELPG tour from the north east on March 6, 1993.

LMS 'Black Five' 4-6-0 No. 45305 has just passed under the aqueduct and is about to enter Blea Moor tunnel with the Railway Touring Company's 'Waverley' from York on September 9, 2012.

CHAPTER 12

Dent Head-Garsdale

ON THE climb from Settle Junction to Ribblehead and Blea Moor, the line has followed the wide Ribble valley, with the road close by, but emerging from the northern portal of Blea Moor tunnel, the outlook is completely different. The line is now in Dentdale, but not in the valley itself, it is high above it, clinging to the hillside and crossing two deep ravines on tall viaducts. The valley of Dentdale takes its name from the village of Dent, which the railway misses by a good four miles, although a station was built at the closest point and optimistically named Dent.

The Dent Fault cuts across the valley close to the village of Gawthrop, marking a geological boundary between the carboniferous limestone of Deepdale and the Craven Dales to the south and the older Silurian and Ordovician rocks of the Howgill Fells to the north. Emerging from the tunnel, the line crosses the 10 arch 100ft high Dent Head viaduct, which was built between 1869 and 1875 from massive blocks of Dent 'marble', and it crosses over the quarry that produced it. The owners of the quarry, Dent Marble Works received £1300 in compensation for disruption to the business.

A long cutting after Dent Head leads to the even more impressive, but much less accessible 11 arches, 117ft high, 220 yards long, Arten Gill viaduct, the second highest on the line.

This viaduct is also built of massive blocks of Dent 'marble', actually fossilised black limestone, and carries the line over Arten Gill Beck. The 'marble' was popular for use in ornamental masonry and was remarkable for its wealth of fossils. The viaduct's piers are tapered, with prominent springings for the arches. Two sets of widened piers, which are designed to prevent progressive collapse should one of the arches fail, divide the viaduct into sections of two, three and six spans.

The gill is deep and the banks on each side are steep; before the viaduct was commenced there was a 60ft waterfall. Great difficulty was experienced in obtaining a firm foundation for several of the piers, and then they had to be sunk in some cases as much as 55ft. The foundations were, however, eventually laid on the rock.

Under the viaduct is Arten Gill Lane, originally part of the old road from Dentdale to Hawes and its history reflects its use in the life of the community and the local economy. Starting from the small settlement of Stone House in Dentdale, the Arten Gill walled lane rises on to the open moor above and continues on its way eastward to its junction

LMS 'Black Five' 4-6-0 No. 5305 emerges from Blea Moor tunnel on March 8, 1986, with the West Yorkshire Metropolitan County Council 'West Yorkshire Dalesman' from Leeds. This train conveyed a number of politicians and was part of the campaign to save the line, succeeding in attracting considerable publicity in the national press.

Seen from above the tunnel, Class 60 No. 60006 runs south through Dentdale with a test train in 1990. With the rundown of the Settle & Carlisle line, all freight traffic ceased, and apart from occasional engineers' trains, the first 'freight' workings, albeit non revenue-earning, were a series of test trains for the newly-introduced Brush Class 60 Type 5 freight diesels.

The first Jubilee over the S&C for 12 years, LMS 4-6-0 No. 5690 *Leander* crosses Dent Head viaduct with a northbound railtour on April 26, 1980.

Class 47 No. 47488 crosses Arten Gill viaduct with a Leeds-Carlisle train on September 15, 1990. The spoil heaps from excavation of the deep cutting between Arten Gill and Dent Head can clearly be seen on the hillside.

with the Hawes-Ingleton road at Widdale Foot.

The route was mainly used as a drove road to take animals to local farms and markets and to access upland pasture and moorland. It was also used to access the upper fellsides, where coal was mined for local consumption and the local dark limestone was quarried.

Use of the lane declined following the construction of the modern road network between Hawes, Ingleton and Dent in the bottom of the valley, and in recent times Arten Gill had become almost impassable. Running adjacent to a fell and down a steep gill, it had basically become a water course eroded to 6ft deep and 10ft wide, but it has been restored in the biggest single project carried out on the Pennine Bridleway to date. A section of the route has now been transformed into a stable, solid, properly drained track, accessible once more to walkers.

Dent station is about four miles east of the village of Dent and 600ft higher, actually situated at Cowgill. Closed in 1970 and reopened in 1986, it is Britain's highest main line station, 1150ft above sea level. North east of the station are the remains of snow fences created from old railway sleepers which were erected to try and keep snow off the tracks. Unfortunately these were not always successful and in the winters of 1947 and 1963 Dent station became heavily snowbound.

The station buildings are now in private hands and used for upmarket holiday accommodation. In a particularly bleak location, the former stationmaster's house, renovated in 2012, was one of the first houses built in Britain to be fitted with double-glazing.

Dent is in Cumbria, in the valley of Dentdale, but the river is the River Dee, a tributary of the River Lune. It was the birthplace of Adam Sedgwick, widely credited with inventing the science of geology, and commemorated in the village by a block of granite.

The remains of the snow fence can still be seen at Dent.

Dent is famous for its knitters. In the 18th century, both men and women knitted, often while walking to the fields. Their output of hand-knitted gloves and socks was enormous, providing an important supplementary income.

At Cowgill is one of the most remote breweries in Britain – The Dent Brewery, brewer of award-winning ales which can be bought in any of the three pubs in Dent and brewery trips are available.

The steep, winding road road from Dent station to Garsdale is known as the 'Coal Road' due to the small opencast coal mines which were once worked nearby.

After leaving Dent, the line enters a cutting and after a long embankment, leaves Dentdale and enters the 1213 yard Rise Hill Tunnel. Because of its inaccessibility, this tunnel was the last structure to be constructed on the line. Leaving the tunnel, the line is in Garsdale but remains high up the hillside, above the River Clough and the Hawes to Sedburgh road.

From Rise Hill tunnel to Hawes Junction, the line is mainly level and it was on this section at Ling Gill that water troughs were situated in steam days. Constructed by the MR in 1907, they were the highest not only in Britain but in the world.

The engine that brought steam back to the S&C two days earlier, returns south over Arten Gill on March 27, 1978. LNER V2 2-6-2 No. 4771 *Green Arrow* heads SLOA's 'Norfolkman', named as a tribute to the well-known railwayman Dick Hardy who had overseen the return of the engine to steam at Norwich a few years earlier.

Railfreight Petroleum liveried Class 31 No. 31207 crosses Arlen Gill viaduct with a morning Carlisle-Leeds train on September 15, 1990. Dent station can be seen directly above the locomotive.

An up Northern Rail service crosses Arten Gill viaduct on August 26, 2012.

An up train passes Dent on March 31, 2012.

LNER A3 Pacific No.4472 *Flying Scotsman* departs from Dent with a southbound 'Cumbrian Mountain Express' on April 19, 1980. Photo stops at Dent were a feature of railtours at that time, with little other traffic on the line and a leisurely one-way trip with steam. The signalbox was switched out and the station and 'box deserted on a Saturday afternoon.

LMS Princess Royal Pacific No.6201 *Princess Elizabeth* passes Dent on June 3, 2006, with the Railway Touring Company's 'Cumbrian Mountain Express' which it worked from Doncaster to Carlisle. The station building is now in private hands offering upmarket B&B accommodation.

LNER V2 2-6-2 No. 4771 *Green Arrow* has just emerged from the southern portal of Rise Hill tunnel with a southbound 'Cumbrian Mountain Express' and approaches Dent on September 30, 1989.

LNER A3 Pacific No. 4472 *Flying Scotsman* is seen from above the northern portal of Rise Hill tunnel accelerating away from Garsdale on May 16, 1992, returning from Carlisle to York.

LMS Princess Coronation Pacific No. 46229 *Duchess of Hamilton* has just departed from Dent northbound and approaches Rise Hill tunnel on October 29, 1983.

CHAPTER 13

Garsdale-Ais Gill

HAWES JUNCTION, as its name suggests, was a branch diverged to the east to the market town of Hawes, where it made an end-on connection with the North Eastern Railway branch from the East Coast Main Llne at Northallerton through Wensleydale.

This branch line was closed to passengers in 1959, but remained in use for limestone and military trains from the eastern end to Redmire until the 1990s; and the section from Leeming Bar to Redmire is now operated by the Wensleydale Railway, whose long term aim is to extend from Redmire right through to connect with the S&C once again.

Award plaque at Garsdale station.

Hawes Junction station once boasted a waiting room where Anglican church services were held. From 1900 it was named Hawes Junction and Garsdale but became just Garsdale in 1932. Like most stations it was closed between 1970 and 1986. The main settlement in Garsdale was several miles to the west, beyond Rise Hill tunnel, but the MR built 16 railway cottages for its employees when the line opened and a further six cottages were added near to the Moorcock Inn soon afterwards. This became the more important settlement in the area, the village of Garsdale now being regarded as being adjacent to the station which bears the name. The population of the parish recorded in the 2011 census was 191 but was estimated at 201 in 2019.

Garsdale has 18 working farms, but because of the high annual rainfall of up to 100in, crops other than hay and silage are almost impossible, so all farms are stock rearing.

In steam days, Garsdale had a turntable with a wall of sleepers around it to prevent locomotives being blown round by strong winds, as allegedly happened in 1900. The turntable is now in operation at Keighley on the Keighley & Worth Valley Railway but the original turntable pit can still be seen east of

Garsdale station. The present signalbox on the platform was built in 1910 to replace two earlier 'boxes.

Hawes Junction is unfortunately synonymous with one of Britain's worst railway accidents, which occurred on Christmas Eve 1910. It was a busy railway centre and the signalman on duty, who was called Sutton, forgot that he had a pair of light engines waiting at his Down (northbound) starting signal on the main line to return to their shed at Carlisle.

They were still waiting there when the signalman set the road for the Down Scotch Express. When the signal cleared, the light engines set off in front of the express into the same block section. Since the light engines were travelling at low speed from a stand at Hawes Junction and the following express was travelling at high speed, a collision was inevitable. The express caught the light engines just after Moorcock tunnel and was almost completely derailed.

Casualties were made worse by the telescoping of the wooden-bodied coaches, which caught fire, fed by the gas from lights leaking from ruptured pipes. Twelve people were killed.

Another driver saw what had happened and told the signalman. Signalman Sutton refused to believe him until he telephoned the next signalbox at Ais Gill to ask whether the two light engines had gone through. When the Ais Gill signalman replied that none had been offered to him, nor had the express passed, Sutton was quoted as saying: "I am afraid I have wrecked the Scotch Express."

Beyond Garsdale, the line sweeps round to the north over Dandry Mire viaduct and enters the short Moorcock tunnel, named after the nearby inn. At the head of Wensleydale and originally called the Guide Post Inn, the Moorcock Inn is 1050ft above sea level making it one of North Yorkshire's highest pubs.

Emerging from the tunnel, the line crosses the five-arch Lunds viaduct and passes under a footbridge, a surprising feature bearing in mind only one station on the line was provided with such a luxury by the Midland Railway.

The River Ure rises only a short distance to the east, on Lunds Fell, but the stream in the bottom of the gill becomes the River Eden as it flows down to Mallerstang parallel to the railway, a short distance further north being Hell Gill Bridge, the turning

Every dog has his day

AT GARSDALE station stands a statue of Ruswarp, a collie. Ruswarp belonged to Graham Nuttall, the first secretary of the Friends of the Settle-Carlisle Line, which was formed to campaign against the proposed closure of the line. Ruswarp's pawprint was put on his own objection as a fare-paying passenger.

Just after the line was finally saved in 1989, Nuttall and Ruswarp went missing in the Welsh mountains in January 1990. On April 7 that year a lone walker found Nuttall's body by a mountain stream. Nearby was Ruswarp, so weak that the 14-year-old dog had to be carried off the mountain, having stayed with his master's body for 11 winter weeks. He survived long enough to attend Nuttall's funeral.

The statue of Ruswarp at Garsdale station.

Garsdale was traditionally a water stop for steam railtours. LNER A3 Pacific No. 4472 *Flying Scotsman* has its tender topped up as Scotrail Class 47 No. 47644 passes with an Up train on May 4, 1987. Better facilities and a more reliable supply at Appleby plus much tighter timings now make a Garsdale top-up inconvenient. Being so near the summit it is unnecessary anyway; the engine will use very little water on the mostly downhill run from Garsdale in either direction.

point. Hell Gill Bridge is a single arch of stone and dates from 1825, replacing an earlier structure, and a small stone in one of its parapets is thought to be an old boundary stone between Yorkshire and what was then Westmorland.

Hell Gill now marks the county boundary of Yorkshire and Cumbria and the edge of the Yorkshire Dales National Park. The narrow neck of land lying between the gill, which becomes the River Eden and flows out to the Solway Firth, and the River Ure, which flows eastwards to the North Sea, lies on the watershed of Britain, the true divide between east and west.

Shotlock Hill is an apparently unnecessary 106-yard tunnel. The line has one last climb, at 1-in-165 from the entrance to Moorcock tunnel to Shotlock Hill where the gradient eases to 1-in-330 for the last mile to Ais Gill Summit. This is 1169ft above sea level, the summit of the line and the highest point on the main line railway system in England.

From Ais Gill it's downhill virtually all the way to Carlisle, and time for the fireman to relax.

LNER K4 2-6-0 No. 61994 *The Great Marquess* crosses Dandry Mire viaduct with a northbound Statesman Rail 'Fellsman' from Lancaster to Carlisle on August 8, 2012.

LMS Princess Coronation Pacific No. 46229 *Duchess of Hamilton* crosses Dandry Mire viaduct just after departing from a water stop at Garsdale with a northbound 'Cumbrian Mountain Pullman' on October 29, 1983.

Class 31 No. 31416 has just come off Dandry Mire viaduct with a morning Carlisle-Leeds service on September 21, 1990, and approaches Hawes Junction just before arriving at Garsdale.

LMS 'Black Five' 4-6-0 No. 5407 performs a photographic runpast for train passengers on a 'Cumbrian Mountain Pullman' over Dandry Mire viaduct on May 2, 1981.

The signalbox on the platform at Garsdale.

DBS Class 66 No. 66162 passes Garsdale with the daily Carlisle-Crewe engineers' train on August 4, 2012.

LNER A4 Pacific No. 60009 *Union of South Africa* crosses Lunds viaduct northbound on May 2, 1992.

LMS Jubilee 4-6-0 No. 5593 *Kolhapur* emerges from Moorcock tunnel and crosses Lunds viaduct on March 21, 1987.

A Class 47 crosses Lunds viaduct and is about to enter Moorcock tunnel with a Carlisle-Leeds train on June 20, 1987. Wild Boar Fell dominates the horizon.

MS Princess Coronation Pacific No. 6233 *Duchess of Sutherland* emerges from Shotlock Hill tunnel with the Royal Train conveying HRH Prince Charles to Kirkby Stephen on March 22, 2005.

LNER V2 2-6-2 No.4771 *Green Arrow* has just emerged from Shotlock Hill tunnel and is on the last lap to Ais Gill summit northbound on September 16, 1989.

Having just topped Ais Gill summit, SR unrebuilt Bulleid West Country Pacific No. 34092 *City of Wells* approaches Shotlock Hill tunnel southbound with an early morning railtour from Appleby to York promoted by the Appleby Round Table on September 26, 1987.

CHAPTER 14

The Right Kind of Snow

THERE HAVE been some severe winters recently in spite of global warming, but in the Dales none have compared with 1947 when Dent was snowbound for two months, or 1963.

Even in the worst winter conditions since then, there has been little disruption to train services and even the majority of steam workings in the preservation era scheduled to run in the worst of the winter weather have run as advertised, in many cases treating passengers and onlookers to some of the finest sights to be seen on Britain's railways.

This really is a railway, not a scene from a parallel universe in which the Settle and Carlisle line was closed long ago after all. On January 18, 2010, even when the railway tracks were barely visible, the trains kept running, albeit at 20mph, as viewed from the cab of a train ploughing through the snow. NETWORK RAIL

MR Compound 4-4-0 No. 1000 and LMS Jubilee 4-6-0 No. 5690 *Leander* round the curve into Rise Hill tunnel with a southbound 'Cumbrian Mountain Express' on February 12, 1983.

LMS Royal Scot 4-6-0 No. 46115 *Scots Guardsman* passes through the cutting between Blea Moor and the tunnel with Past-Time Rail's 'Cumbrian Fellsman' on February 7, 2009.

In Christmas card conditions, SR King Arthur 4-6-0 No. 777 Sir Lamiel climbs away from Horton-in-Ribblesdale with the Humberside Locomotive Preservation Group/SLOA 'Santa Steam Special' from Hull which the National Collection-owned engine worked from Leeds to Carlisle on December 27, 1984.

CHAPTER 15

Diversions

The Settle & Carlisle line has been a useful diversionary route for West Coast Main Line trains when there has been engineering work or derailments on the line over Shap. This of course would only have applied after the Grouping of 1923, and even then, WCML trains would often have been diverted north of Preston via Blackburn, Hellifield, Settle Junction, and Ingleton to rejoin the WCML at Low Gill.

In fact there is little evidence of the wholesale diversion of WCML expresses via the S&C in steam days, and it is only since the 1970s that BR regularly sent Sunday or weekend WCML trains via the S&C, bringing the English Electric Class 50s to the line.

It was not only the WCML services that made use of the line; throughout 1979, the S&C saw East Coast Main Line trains as a result of the collapse of Penmanshiel tunnel north of Berwick-upon-Tweed. While most ECML trains simply ran from Newcastle to Edinburgh via Carlisle and Carstairs, the Newcastle-Carlisle line could not accommodate all the traffic and some trains ran from Doncaster via Leeds and Carlisle.

Of course, having played such a vital part in keeping the traffic flowing after one of BR's most serious problems, it was just a couple of years later that BR announced that the Settle & Carlisle was to close. The run-down of the line over the next few years saw many signalboxes closed and the capacity of the line became seriously limited.

The WCML over Shap had been electrified in 1974 and it was therefore necessary to find diesel locomotives to haul WCML expresses if they ran via the S&C. As a result WCML diversions became fairly infrequent, but there have been occasional instances where there has been the wholesale diversion of all trains, for one or more weekends. March 1989 for example saw the S&C running at full capacity at weekends with a procession of Class 47-hauled expresses in each direction. At this time there was no S&C freight traffic and WCML freights were sent via the Cumbrian Coast, Carnforth and Settle Junction.

In more recent times, Privatisation has made the diversion of trains more problematic because driver route knowledge is now far more limited. Virgin Trains held the West Coast franchise from 1997 to December 2019 and its drivers did not 'sign the road' over the S&C, so the company tended to replace trains with buses when the WCML was closed (since December 2019, the franchise has been held by Avanti West Coast).

Class 57/3 No. 57309 curves off Ribblehead viaduct on April 29, 2006, dragging Class 390 Pendolino unit No. 390047 *Virgin Atlantic* (since renamed *CLIC Sargent*) on a Glasgow Central-Euston service diverted from the usual WCML route due to engineering works. FRED KERR

The spring of 2007 saw a series of diversions and many Virgin services were worked by diesel Voyager units and a few of these used the S&C for several weekends. Perhaps more interesting though was the use of Virgin's Class 57 'Thunderbirds' to drag Pendolino units over the line.

Diverted freight traffic can also be of interest with the Daventry-Grangemouth Tesco container train sometimes using the line, or the Teesside-Shap limestone train running via Leeds and Carlisle instead of Newcastle.

Class 47 No. 47544 heads a Down West Coast Main Line express over Sheriff Brow viaduct in March 1989.

A pair of Class 221 Voyager units, No. 221137 *Mayflower Pilgrims* and No. 221105 *William Baffin*, curve through Langcliffe on April 14, 2007, with a Plymouth-Glasgow Central service diverted from the WCML. FRED KERR

CHAPTER 16

Railtours

THE SETTLE & Carlisle line has always been a popular destination for railtours, many originating from London. Carlisle is feasible for a day trip from London and in the early days of steam preservation while steam infrastructure still existed it was just about possible to run with steam throughout from King's Cross to Carlisle and back in a day.

While steam trains have been the highprofile passenger workings on the line in recent years, there are diesel-hauled railtours most weeks throughout the year, ranging from the 'trackbashers' multi-engine high mileage tours to the top end wine-and-dine experiences offered by Venice Simplon-Orient-Express', 'Northern Belle' or the 'Royal Scotsman'.

The run-down of the Settle & Carlisle line and its ultimate reprieve in the 1980s coincided with BR's rail blue era and it would have been a rare sight in those days to have seen a train of anything other than corporate blue and grey stock on the line. The last regular locomotivehauled trains ran with blue and grey stock and the first steam railtours on the line ran with admittedly longer trains, but in just the same livery.

Changes were afoot though and as locomotive-hauled coaching stock was rapidly phased out of regular BR service, a dedicated set of coaches was set up exclusively for steam operations by SLOA under the banner of Pullman-Rail. These comprised mainly Metropolitan-Gammell Pullman cars, also in blue and grey but which began to be repainted so that trains of umber and cream became the order of the day. However, problems with blue asbestos insulation led to the Pullman's temporary withdrawal and a set of Mk.1 stock was purchased and quickly repainted maroon. With the return of the Pullmans in due course, two sets of privately owned stock in 1960s livery became available for steam tours.

In the run-up to the privatisation of BR in 1994, first came Sectorisation. Diverted WCML expresses in particular started to feature InterCity 'raspberry ripple' livery and as most main line steam trains came under the control of InterCity, this livery came to be seen interspersed with the more traditional Pullman colours.

Other sets of privately owned coaches came to be assembled, carrying a variety of liveries, some more attractive and authentic than others. The Pullmans though were withdrawn from service and replaced by a BR set of Mk.1 stock which was painted into traditional 1960s maroon livery. No sooner was painting completed though than the set was

Class 50s were once regular on the line but had all moved to the Western Region by 1980, while High Speed Trains have never been frequent visitors so to see both at once was certainly unusual. Nos. 50008 *Thunderer* and 50034 *Furious* on Pathfinder Tours' 'Fellsman' from Taunton meet an HST set on Hertfordshire Railtours' 'Settle & Carlisle 125' at Birkett on January 30, 1988.

painted again into 1950s carmine and cream, then back into maroon. By now this set was ageing, and in the ownership of Riviera Trains, and it became mixed with vehicles in SR green, WR chocolate and cream or even Riviera Trains' house colours of blue and cream.

In addition, we briefly saw the 'Pilkington' set of Mk.1s in green livery, the 'Lakeland Pullman' in crimson and gold and vehicles from the short-lived Wessex Trains Mk.2 set.

A rare visitor to the Settle & Carlisle route on July 31, 2010, was preserved Class 52 dieselhydraulic D1015 *Western Champion*, seen approaching the summit of Ais Gill with the return working of Pathfinder Tours' 'Western Fellsrunner' railtour from Westbury to Carlisle. FRED KERR

A Class 47 heads the former Manchester Pullman stock downhill through Baron Wood on May 16, 1992.

Preserved by the Class 40 Preservation Society Class 40 D345 crosses Ais Gill viaduct with Pathfinder Tours' 'Pennine Fellsman' on July 12, 2003.

CLASS 40

THE SETTLE & Carlisle line was only slowly dieselised by BR. Although the first big main line diesels appeared in 1958, in the shape of the English Electric Type 4 and BR/Sulzer 'Peak' 1Co-Co1s, the S&C was not seen as a priority to receive these in place of the steam engines. As steam was phased out over the next 10 years, the West Riding sheds of the North Eastern Region retained steam until September 1967, and Carlisle in the London Midland Region did not see full dieselisation until December 1967. While these two areas had steam, the S&C was still at least partially a steam-worked railway.

Once it became totally diesel-operated, any LMR or NER-allocated diesels could appear but the surviving expresses tended to be monopolised by the Class 45 and 46 'Peaks', allocated to Holbeck shed at Leeds. Class 40s had been largely displaced from premier WCML work by the Brush/Sulzer Class 47s and were a common sight on the heavier S&C freight workings.

The 'Peaks' largely disappeared with the end of S&C express workings in 1982 and Brush Class 31 and 47 diesels were seen on most of the locomotive-hauled trains. The Class 40s, though, soldiered on and in a popular move with enthusiasts, the class staged a remarkable comeback in the shape of just one engine.

The pioneer Class 40 No.40122 was withdrawn from service in August 1981 and despite much persuasion the National Railway Museum did not want it. It was not considered practical to preserve it privately but a campaign by enthusiasts persuaded BR to reinstate it.

It was rebuilt as an apprentice training exercise at Toton depot and returned to service in BR green livery in April 1983, also numbered D200, allocated to Carlisle depot.

Naturally it was in demand for enthusiast railtours but when not required elsewhere it had a daily passenger diagram on the out and back Carlisle-Leeds passenger working, taking it over the S&C twice a day for the next five years. When finally withdrawn, the NRM changed its policy and agreed to accept it for preservation.

D200 heads the afternoon Leeds-Carlisle train past Sheriff Brow on June 20, 1987.

Class 47 No. 47809 works the universally despised Pilkington-liveried Mk.1 set over Ais Gill on May 16, 1992. These coaches did occasionally feature in steam railtours.

LMS Princess Royal Pacific No. 46203 *Princess Margaret Rose* storms towards Birkett tunnel on August 24, 1991.

CHAPTER 17

London Midland & Scottish Railway

AS PART of the LMSR, it was that company's engines which will always be associated with the S&C. From the turn of the century, the Midland Compound 4-4-0s monopolised express workings with 2P 4-4-0s on the stopping trains and 3F and 4F 0-6-0s on the goods, many trains of course being doubleheaded in the tradition of the MR's small engine policy.

The LMS built rather bigger engines and by the mid-1930s, Stanier's 'Black Five' and Jubilee 4-6-0s had taken charge of the heavier trains, while the SF 2-8-0s were increasingly seen on goods workings, with 'foreigners' such as LNWR Claughtons also appearing.

Only in BR days, after displacement from some WCML and trans-Pennine workings, were the

In LMS post-war black Livery, No. 6233 *Duchess of Sutherland* has just emerged from Birkett tunnel on August 28, 2010. PETER AINSWORTH

LMS Stanier mogul No. 2968 tops Ais Gill southbound in wintry conditions on January 4, 1997. JOHN WHITELEY

Royal Scot 4-6-0s seen regularly on the line, and the Midland Compounds still played their part, particularly piloting the heavier expresses. The line was under London Midland Region control in BR days, the border with the North Eastern Region being between Skipton and Hellifield, but LMS traction was supplemented by increasing numbers of BR Standard types plus even some LNER Pacifics in the early 1960s. LMS and BR Standard engines were in sole charge by 1967 though.

In the preservation era, it was not until 1980 that an LMS engine returned to the S&C, in the shape of 'Black Five' No. 5305 and Jubilee No. 5690 *Leander*, a Bristol-based engine in steam days.

The S&C has seen 'Black Fives' Nos. 44767, 44871, 45305, 45407 and 44932 and 45231, all of which were north-western engines in 1967/68, but in the case of the latter two have only been seen on the line in more recent years.

All three active preserved Jubilees have returned to the line; No. 5593 *Kolhapur* briefly in 1987, and the double chimneyed No. 45596 *Bahamas* for a few years from 1989, while No. 5690 has been fairly regular since 1980 and being based at Carnforth is likely to be seen frequently in the future along with its fellow Barry scrapyard occupant, one-time Bristol-based No. 45699 *Galatea* – which made its railtour debut on May 19, 2013.

Stanier Pacifics were synonymous with Carlisle but stuck firmly to the West Coast Main Line and were only seen on the S&C in rare cases of emergency diversions. Of the Princess Royals, No. 6201 *Princess Elizabeth*, withdrawn from Carlisle in 1962 and one of the first main line engines to be privately preserved, did not find its way to the S&C until 1980, and then only on a very brief foray to the north, but after the Princess Margaret Rose Locomotive Trust's No. 46203 *Princess Margaret Rose* made its first appearance in June 1991, both Princesses came to be seen regularly, sometimes even on the same day.

The celebrated Princess Coronation Pacifics' appearances were rare in steam days. In the preservation era, No. 46229 *Duchess of Hamilton* made the line its own for many years, and was arguably the most popular engine among enthusiasts. It did

On the first of many runs over the S&C, David Smith's LMS 8F 2-8-0 No. 48151 emerges from Blea Moor tunnel into Dentdale on June 25, 1988.

not get off to a good start though, stalling at Langcliffe on November 1, 1980, and having to be pushed by a Class 40. The problem was leaves on the line during the autumn leaf fall season, with by then virtually no heavy trains using the line to keep the railheads clean.

After No. 46229's retirement in 1998, No. 6233 *Duchess of Sutherland* soon took its place but did not have quite the same following. Changes in its livery though have revived interest and the engine has brought us the sight of not only an LMS maroon Duchess, but an LMS black one and a BR green one.

It is hard to compare engine performance on the line, with steam being limited to 75mph generally and all trains over the S&C being limited to 60mph. No. 46229 is widely credited with consistently recording the fastest runs from Appleby to Ais Gill summit, but other engines have at least equalled its performance, if not on such a regular basis.

The National Railway Museum's preserved MR Compound 4-4-0 No. 1000 reappeared twice in the snow in 1983, to pilot No. 5690 in a memorable pair of tours. In 1988, an 8F was seen on passenger duties in the shape of No. 48151 owned by David Smith. It was not fully appreciated just how significant this was but David Smith's West Coast Railway Company has spearheaded the return to steam on the S&C in quantity in recent years, with his 8F playing a significant role. The other 8F, the Severn Valley Railway's No. 48773 just did a couple of trips, doubleheading with No. 45407 in 1999.

Another engine primarily designed for goods traffic but which was a popular main line performer for several years was the SVRbased Stanier mogul No. 2968 which did a northbound train in December 1996, returning south in the snow the following month.

In 2008 though we finally saw a 'Scot'. No. 46115 *Scots Guardsman* hauled its final railtour for BR over the line in February 1965. It was purchased for preservation and steamed briefly in 1978/9. After two changes of ownership, West Coast finally returned it to steam in BR green in July 2008, its first main line outing being over the S&C, since when it has become one of the most popular engines to be seen on the line.

CHAPTER 18

LNER Steam

THE S&C essentially ran from Leeds to Carlisle, and the sheds responsible for most long-distance workings in steam days were Leeds Holbeck, and Carlisle Durran Hill until 1936, then Upperby. Naturally Midland and LMS engines were always going to predominate but both Leeds and Carlisle did play host to engines of LNER pedigree. In the very late stages of steam working, one or two LNER classes briefly found themselves working in what would traditionally be regarded as foreign territory.

And so in the early 1960s, the S&C regularly saw LNER Peppercorn A1 and A2 and Gresley A3 Pacifics. In the preservation era, the return of steam traction to the line at Easter 1978 came in the shape of an LNER engine, V2 2-6-2 No. 4771 *Green Arrow*. It was followed the same year by A3 No. 4472 *Flying Scotsman* and A4 Pacific No. 4498 *Sir Nigel Gresley*.

The streamlined A4 Pacifics were certainly a rare sight on the line in steam days but No. 4498 had made its first trip in preservation over the S&C on April 1, 1967, having been overhauled at Crewe Works. It was followed on July 17 that year by No. 60019 *Bittern's* second trip in preservation, but this engine's initial return to main line service was very brief. No. 4498 though has been seen much more consistently and once it had rejoined the action in 1978, it played a prominent part in early 'Cumbrian Mountain Expresses' workings, based at Carnforth.

A third A4, John Cameron's No. 60009 *Union of South Africa*, traditionally a Scottish engine both before and after preservation, eventually visited England on March 31, 1984, its first train south of the border being a southbound 'CME'. And yet another A4, the record-breaking No. 4468 *Mallard* worked just two trains over the line during its three-year return to active service, the first one in June 1988. Its second and final one sadly was not its finest hour, stalling just before Birkett tunnel.

K1 2-6-0 No. 2005 has been a fairly regular visitor to the line since 1981, although it has been heavily committed to service on the West Highland line at Fort William in recent years. Another LNER mogul, Gresley K4 No. 3442 *The Great Marquess*, one of the first preserved steam engines to run on the main line in the early 1960s, made a couple of appearances on the line in the late 1980s, but now also in the ownership of John Cameron, and in BR livery as No. 61994, saw regular use on West Coast Railway's trips in the summer of 2012, matching the performance of rather larger engines. B1 No. 1264

An unusual type of engine for the route but one which has been seen quite regularly since 1981, LNER K1 2-6-0 No. 2005 works upgrade away from Horton in Ribblesdale with the North Eastern Locomotive Preservation Group's 'Northumbrian Mountain Pullman', which it worked from Hellifield to Middlesbrough via Carlisle on March 20, 1983.

LNER A4 Pacific No. 60009 *Union of South Africa* passes Blea Moor with a 'Cumbrian Mountain Express' on April 20, 1984.

On the last run of a limited main line programme, LNER A4 Pacific No. 4468 *Mallard* struggles uphill at Birkett on August 27, 1988. A few yards further on, the record-breaking Pacific stalled, due to a build-up of ash in its smokebox.

made just one run after its restoration from Barry scrapyard condition, piloting LMS 8F No. 48151.

An eagerly awaited return to main line service in the preservation era was Peppercorn A2 No. 60532 *Blue Peter*, which with its 6ft 2in driving wheels is nominally Britain's most powerful Pacific. Operated then by the North Eastern Locomotive Preservation Group, its performances over the S&C in the 1990s did not disappoint. When the A2 made its appearance on the line, no one was taking any bets on whether we would one day see an A1 Pacific, but the A1 Steam Locomotive Trust had made a start on constructing the 50th member of a class which was made extinct in 1966. In 2008, the brand new No. 60163 *Tornado* steamed at Darlington, and on October 3, 2009, it made its first run over the S&C, though sadly its appearances on the line since have been rather sporadic.

Both *Green Arrow* and *Flying Scotsman* proved to be two of the most regularly seen LNER engines for many years, but the A3 was sold soon after its 1988/9 Australian trip, and although eventually returned to main line service after one of the most thorough and expensive overhauls of any preserved steam engine, the double chimneyed A3 stayed in the south and was never seen on the S&C. Now in the hands of the NRM, *Flying Scotsman* underwent an extensive £4.5m overhaul lasting a full decade – from 2006 to 2016 – finally re-emerging for testing in January 2016.

Green Arrow was retired in 2007, needing the complete replacement of its cylinder block, a repair which is unlikely to be sanctioned. Of the A4 Pacifics, No. 60009, overhauled at Crewe in 2012, continued in regular service until the expiry of its boiler ticket (following a 12-month extension) in March 2020. No. 60007, occasionally seen on the S&C, was being overhauled at the time of writing following the expiry of its boiler ticket in September 2015. No. 60019 was an infrequent visitor to S&C metals during the early 2010s but was withdrawn for a major overhaul in 2015.

CHAPTER 19

Great Western

GREAT WESTERN engines were simply unknown on the S&C in steam days for two reasons. They have always been considered incompatible with the rest of the railway system, because of the railway's broad gauge origins which resulted in its standard gauge express engines still being built to rather bigger proportions than those of other lines.

GWR engines were geographically remote from the S&C anyway and very rarely strayed outside their home territory at all. Yet on the last day of BR steam working over the S&C from the West Riding, preserved GWR 4-6-0 No. 7029 *Clun Castle* worked a railtour from Peterborough to Carlisle on September 30, 1967, which returned to Peterborough with preserved LNER A4 Pacific No. 4498 *Sir Nigel Gresley*.

The following day, the itinerary was repeated with the engines working the opposite legs but No. 7029 came to grief. Some cotton waste found its way into the tender and into various important bits of pipework. It only made it to Leeds where a diesel took over.

Since *Clun Castle's* pioneering run, with problems which could not be blamed on the engine, GWR engines have continued to have mixed fortunes. No less than 27 years later, a single-chimneyed Castle, No. 5029 *Nunney Castle's* first northbound run over the S&C was extremely laboured and its southbound performance a month later was worse, slipping to a stand at Kirkby Stephen and requiring diesel assistance, resulting in a two hour delay.

Although Castles were found to fit not only the S&C loading gauge, but lines such as the WCML needed to get there, even after electrification, the same could not be said for the GWR's premier express class, the Kings. Although No. 6000 *King George V* had spearheaded the Return to Steam on BR in 1971/2, the class was heavily restricted even within the GW system in steam days, and it was still found to be impossible for it to run anywhere on other regions.

However, the owning society of No. 6024 *King Edward I* had a solution; by shortening its chimney and making a few other modifications, it was made to fit the loading gauge of most main lines. Unfortunately its 1998/9 encounters with both the S&C and Shap were worse than No. 5029's, although not helped by the weather. Like No. 5029, the King also stalled at Kirkby Stephen on the southbound run, blamed on air entering the smoke box.

A smaller GWR 4-6-0 No. 5972 *Olton Hall* was bought from Barry scrapyard by David Smith in

GWR 4-6-0 No. 5972 *Olton Hall* heads past Selside with 21st Century Trains' Christmas shopping special from Hellifield to Carlisle on December 4, 1999. JOHN SHUTTLEWORTH

GWR 4-6-0 No. 5043 *Earl of Mount Edgcumbe* storms past Helwith Bridge with Vintage Trains' 'Pride of Swindon' tour from Tyseley on October 16, 2010. ALAN WEAVER

GWR 4-6-0 No. 5029 *Nunney Castle* is on the last lap of the northbound climb to Ais Gill summit with a Swindon-Carlisle railtour on February 12, 1994. FRED KERR

1981 and restoration commenced at Horbury. It was completed at Carnforth when West Coast took over the shed and made an unannounced first run over the S&C on May 22, 1999, where it coped well with shorter trains appropriate to a class 5, but did fall foul of the GW gauging problem when a cylinder scraped a platform at Carlisle.

Shortly afterwards of course it was transformed into *Hogwarts Castle* and while it was still certified for main line use it regularly travelled to Euston, King's Cross and Fort William for Harry Potter filming purposes, with no apparent gauging problems, yet Halls are now out of gauge on so much of the WR that their appearances there are becoming infrequent. No. 5972 worked its last railtours in 2014 and has been on static display at Warner Bros. Studio Tour London – The Making of Harry Potter, near Watford, since 2015.

Swindon's reputation in later years was rescued by another double-chimneyed Castle from Tyseley, No. 5043 *Earl of Mount Edgcumbe*. Having first run out and back from Crewe in October 2010, it made an unusual doubleheader in March 2012, teaming up with LMS Pacific *Princess Elizabeth*. The Pacific's failure at Carlisle after the northbound run over Shap resulted in another solo run by the Castle over Ais Gill, with a similar first class performance.

CHAPTER 20

Southern Steam

SOUTHERN RAILWAY steam engines were unknown on the S&C in steam days being allocated south of London and rarely straying far beyond the boundaries of the Southern Region even in BR days. Railtours taking engines far off the beaten track became increasingly popular towards the end of steam though and on June 13, 1964, Merchant Navy Pacific No. 35012 *United States Line* worked the RCTS 'Solway Ranger', handling the Leeds-Carlisle leg via Carnforth and Shap, returning over the S&C.

The preservation era has not only seen a variety of SR steam engines but some have become quite at home on the line. Another Merchant Navy, the preserved No. 35028 *Clan Line* was seen in the first year of the return to steam in 1978 and returned for a couple of trips in 1989.

Three remarkable Southern engines ran on the line in 1981-2, all of which became regular sights throughout the 1980s. Many engines put aside by BR for 'official' preservation in the 1960s were simply stored away from public view for many years, mainly at Preston Park at Brighton, Stratford works and Hellifield shed.

The opening of the National Railway Museum at York in 1975 provided the incentive to get these engines restored and on view, and the NRM quickly proved that it was keen to be involved in steaming engine in its care if possible and was prepared to loan its engines to established preservation organisations.

And so in late 1978, *Flying Scotsman* towed the rusty old SR 4-6-0 No. 30850 *Lord Nelson* to Carnforth for restoration. Returned to steam just in time to appear at the 1980 Rainhill cavalcade, its first encounter with the S&C was unusual. Having worked the Carnforth-Hellifield leg of a 'Cumbrian Mountain Express', it found itself having to shunt a failed diesel and its cement train off the main line at Settle Junction.

Another National Collection SR 4-6-0, King Arthur No. 777 *Sir Lamiel* went on loan to the Humberside Locomotive Preservation Group which restored it to working order at Hull. Both SR 4-6-0s proved to be very capable performers in the northern fells, but *Lord Nelson's* initial return to steam was relatively brief, its boiler requiring virtual replacement.

The first unrebuilt Bulleid Pacific to be restored to steam from Barry scrapyard condition was West Country No. 34092 *City of Wells*, on the Keighley & Worth Valley Railway in 1980. Because of the type's

Bulleid West Country Pacific No. 34027 *Taw Valley* passes Blea Moor northbound on December 14, 1991.

SR 4-6-0 No. 850 *Lord Nelson* crosses Ais Gill viaduct with a southbound 'CME' on March 3, 1984.

Running without smoke deflectors, SR King Arthur 4-6-0 No. 777 *Sir Lamiel* runs through Dentdale between Arten Gill and Dent Head on May 26, 1990.

unconventional design, BR was reluctant to accept it for main line operation at first, but having proved itself on the KWVR, it was accepted on to the main line and was one of the most frequent S&C performers in the 1980s. The only rebuilt Bulleid Light Pacific to have been seen so far though has been another well-travelled West Country, No. 34027 *Taw Valley*, while another unrebuilt example, Battle of Britain No. 34067 *Tangmere* was seen occasionally during the early 2010s before its withdrawal for overhaul in 2016.

It has not only been the Southern's express engines tackling the 'Long Drag', even a Class 6 goods engine has made an appearance. S15 4-6-0 No. 828, restored at Eastleigh, did a couple of trips in 1994.

CHAPTER 21

BR Standard

BRITISH RAILWAYS introduced its Standard range of steam locomotive designs in 1951, starting with a Class 7 two-cylindered Pacific No. 70000 *Britannia*. Designed by Robert Riddles, a former LMS man from Crewe, and based largely on LMS practice, the Standards were widely spread across the BR system.

As steam became concentrated in the north west in the mid-1960s and the Standards were the newest locomotives and designed to be easiest to maintain, many sheds which had workings over the S&C found themselves with increasing numbers of Standard classes.

The Class 6 Clan Pacifics allocated to Carlisle were used on S&C stopping trains, 9F 2-10-0s from Lancashire and Merseyside had regular workings on the heaviest freights, and the 5MT and 4MT 4-6-0s could be seen frequently. The Britannia Pacifics brought the curtain down on S&C steam as virtually the whole class became concentrated at the two Carlisle sheds by 1967, and even those that were not at 12A Kingmoor or 12B Upperby were at other north western sheds such as Newton Heath in Manchester which still sent them over Ais Gill on occasions.

No. 70013 *Oliver Cromwell* not only took the 'Fifteen Guinea Special' north on August 11, 1968, but returned light engine in the evening, the last-ever BR-owned steam engine to top Ais Gill. But the next big green Standard to be seen on the line was not to be for another 10 years when 9F 2-10-0 No. 92220 *Evening Star* worked out and back on May 13, 1978.

It was still many more years before any Britannia reappeared and in the meantime, the unthinkable happened and the unique 8P Pacific No. 71000 *Duke of Gloucester* made an S&C appearance before No. 70000 and while No. 70013 was still incarcerated in Norfolk.

The history of the big Standards is quite involved, three originally being scheduled for preservation as part of the National Collection, No. 70000 by virtue of being the first Standard, No. 71000 because of its Caprotti valve gear and No. 92220 as the last steam engine built by British Railways.

However, a change of plan saw one cylinder and valve gear removed from No. 71000 for preservation but sectioned, and the remains sent for scrap. Both Nos. 70000 and 92220 were in poor condition when withdrawn and deteriorated further while in store, but No. 92220 was given a cosmetic overhaul at Crewe, possibly in error.

The circumstances of No. 70013's preservation were a little mysterious at the time but it was

BR Standard Pacific No. 70000 *Britannia* leaves Moorcock tunnel and crosses Lunds viaduct with UK Railtours 'Cumbrian Mountain Express' on March 3, 2012. PHIL JONES

quickly spirited away to Bressingham in Norfolk and in view of it having apparently become part of the National Collection, the authorities decided to dispose of No. 70000, which was bought for private preservation, returning to steam in 1978.

Evening Star was placed on loan to the Keighley & Worth Valley Railway which quickly put it back in steam while the derelict remains of *Duke of Gloucester* were acquired for preservation from Barry scrapyard in 1974. The seemingly impossible project to rebuild it succeeded and the Duke beat both Britannias to conquer the Long Drag once again.

No. 70000 was only a year behind, but it still took years of often acrimonious argument and negotiation before No. 70013 was recognised as properly being in the control of the National Railway Museum. It was restored at the Great Central

An easterly wind and some smoky coal do their best to obliterate the train as BR Standard 8P Pacific No. 71000 *Duke of Gloucester* makes the climb towards Birkett tunnel on June 1, 1991.

Railway in the nick of time to haul the 40th anniversary rerun of '1T57' in August 2008.

BR 4MT 2-6-4T No. 80080 took part in a month-long series of crew training trips, when it worked four-coach Carlisle to Kirkby Stephen stopping trains in early 1993, it also worked a shortened 'Cumbrian Mountain Express' in driving rain one Saturday. The tender version, in the shape of No. 76079 has also been seen occasionally, double-heading with other engines from the Ian Riley stable at Bury.

CHAPTER 22

Carlisle

CARLISLE IS the county town and the largest settlement in the county of Cumbria, situated 10 miles south of the Scottish border, with a population of 75,306 in 2011 – estimated at 74,889 in 2019. Popularly known as the Border City and part of Cumberland prior to the 1974 local government reorganisation, Carlisle today is the main cultural, commercial and industrial centre for north Cumbria.

Although much of the ancient history of Carlisle is still unclear, it existed before the arrival of the Romans in Britain but it was to become a Roman settlement, established to serve the forts on Hadrian's Wall, and is thought to have burned down during the reign of emperor Nero.

After the Romans left, Hadrian's Wall no longer fulfilled its purpose and by the time of the Norman Conquest of England in 1066, Carlisle was part of Scotland and so did not feature in the Domesday Book of 1086. It was William the Conqueror's son William Rufus who invaded Cumberland and reincorporated it into England in 1092. This led to the construction of Carlisle Castle on the site of the Roman fort, south of the River Eden. The stone-built castle was completed in 1112, together with a keep and city walls. The town gained the status of a diocese in 1122, and the priory became Carlisle Cathedral.

But this was not the end of the matter as Scotland wanted it back. A long-running war continued between England and Scotland and Carlisle changed hands a number of times during the Middle Ages, remaining an important military stronghold no matter who held it.

It was not until the death of Queen Elizabeth I in 1603 that peace began to settle between the two countries.

In 1707 an act of union was passed between England and Scotland, creating Great Britain, and Carlisle finally ceased to be a frontier town, although it did not end its position as a garrison town. It was not quite the end of hostilities of course as the 10th and most recent siege in the city's history

The station takes its name from the Citadel across the road.

LMS Jubilee 4-6-0 No. 5690 *Leander* has just arrived at Carlisle with Kingfisher Railtours' 'Dalesman' from Hellifield on August 17, 2008.

LMS 'Black Five' 4-6-0 No. 44932 climbs towards Carlisle station on former NER metals as a Virgin Pendolino arrives from Euston on August 26, 2012.

took place when Bonnie Prince Charlie took Carlisle during the Jacobite Rising of 1745. It was a shocking experience for the terrified residents but the Jacobites retreated the following year.

The Industrial Revolution brought textile manufacturing to Carlisle in a big way and it developed into a densely populated mill town. This expansion of industry naturally resulted in a big increase in the population as jobs moved from rural farms towards the cities. The city's expansion did not keep pace with the demands of the new population and at one time 25,000 residents only had 5000 houses to live in.

The industrial revolution though, combined with its strategic position, allowed for the development of Carlisle as an important railway town, on the West Coast Main Line and with connections to the east of the country.

Carlisle, although it became an important regional and industrial city was never really a destination in itself but became one of Britain's most important railway crossroads. Unlike Newcastle, 60 miles to the east and a far bigger city but which was served by just the North Eastern Railway, Carlisle became the meeting point of no fewer than seven major railway companies. It boasted a unique array of locomotive and rolling stock liveries in pre-Grouping days that few other centres could hope to equal.

The first railway to reach Carlisle was the Newcastle and Carlisle in 1836, which terminated at a station on London Road, and would eventually become part of the NER. In 1843, the Maryport and Carlisle arrived in the city and in 1846, the Lancaster & Carlisle from the south, followed by the Caledonian Railway from Glasgow in 1847. The West Coast Main Line Anglo-Scottish route was now complete and the two companies jointly built Citadel station in Carlisle.

In the period when winter steam tours were obliged to have an 'Ethel' to provide heating, SR Bulleid Merchant Navy Pacific No. 35028 *Clan Line* passes Petteril Bridge Junction soon after leaving Carlisle with a 'Cumbrian Mountain Express' on January 13, 1989. ETHEL stood for Electric Train Heating Ex-Locomotives and they were Class 25 diesels without traction equipment. Their use was necessary as traditional steam heating was banned after a burst pipe had caused serious injury to a railway employee in an incident in London. It took several years before SLOA was able to provide a Mk. I brake coach converted to a generator car, to replace the 'Ethels' provided by Intercity, vastly improving the appearance of wintertime steam railtours.

In 1853, the Port Carlisle Railway arrived from the north-west, terminating at Canal Junction, and the NER extended its line under the LNWR as the L&C had become, to connect at Canal Junction. The Port Carlisle Railway became part of the North British Railway, whose main line from Edinburgh, the Waverley Route, reached Carlisle in 1861, again at Canal Junction. In 1862, the NER finally gained access to Citadel station by means of a sharply curved and steeply graded connection, and a new chord was also opened to the north to give NBR trains access from Canal Junction. Also represented was the Glasgow & South Western Railway from 1848 with running powers over the Caledonian from Gretna Junction, and the last bit of the jigsaw was the arrival of the Midland over the Settle & Carlisle route in 1875, connecting with the NER at Petteril Bridge Junction.

A problem for the Midland was access to Carlisle station, although this was physically no problem over NER metals. Citadel station though, was owned jointly by the LNWR and Caledonian and the former remained very anti-Midland. But there was a proposal for a merger between the MR and the Glasgow & South Western Railway, and rather than see that happen, the CR granted the MR access to Carlisle, behind the LNWR's back.

Citadel station was built in 1847, in a neo-Tudor style to the designs of William Tite, and expanded and extended in 1875-1876, when the MR arrived. Most of the routes from the station remain in use, the only significant casualty being the NBR's Waverley Route to Edinburgh in 1969.

The National Railway Museum's BR Standard 9F 2-10-0 No. 92220 *Evening Star* drops down from Citadel station as it departs with the 'Border Venturer' on May 13, 1978. A down WCML express is seen approaching the station. This was the third steam train over the S&C route, following *Green Arrow's* pioneering runs six weeks earlier, and was steam hauled from Hellifield to Carlisle and return.

Carlisle Citadel was the meeting point of seven railway companies and was noted for the variety of colourful locomotive and rolling stock liveries in pre-Grouping days. Privatisation has seen something of a revival of this variety with the maroon and Pullman liveries of West Coast Railways' heritage stock contrasting with the FirstTrans-Pennine unit heading for Manchester.

A red Duchess waits to take over its train at the south end of the station in 1981 just as in the late 1950s and early 1960s.

LMS 'Black Five' 4-6-0 No. 44932 awaits departure from Carlisle with Statesman Rail's 'Fellsman' on August 26, 2012.

CHAPTER 23

Carlisle-Langwathby

HAVING LEFT Carlisle and parted with the NER at Petteril Bridge Junction, there was only one way for the line to go: follow the River Eden through Appleby and Kirkby Stephen right to its source near Ais Gill. For many miles the S&C is very close to the LNWR's West Coast Main Line but is climbing at mostly 1-in-132 through rolling farmlands but with the Pennines to the east and the Lake District fells to the south-west.

The first station was at Scotby, the most northerly Midland Railway station; possibly too close to Carlisle to be of use, it closed as early as 1942. It was, however, provided with a medium-sized station building and a waiting shelter on the Up platform. It also had a signalbox but only from 1897 to 1909.

Cumwhinton was also provided with a medium-sized building and although the station was one of the early closures, in 1956, the building has survived as a private residence, and was Grade II listed in 1984. The platforms and former waiting shelter also survive.

A hamlet was established at Cumwhinton by the middle of the 12th century, initially under the name Cumquintina, believed to be named after Saint Quentin. The site also had a manor owned by the Bavin family, who gave it to Lanercost Priory after three generations of ownership.

By 1831, Cumwhinton was a joint township with nearby Cotehill, also in Wetheral parish, and had a population of 472.

Cotehill station was another early closure, in 1952. Nearby were a number of sidings serving brick, tile and plaster works, controlled by a signalbox known as Howe & Co's Sidings. This box, built in 1916, remains open and is the fringe box north of which trains come under the control of Carlisle power 'box. Howe & Company became Cocklake's alabaster works but this was taken over by the Gotham Company of Nottingham.

The line undulates slightly and runs downhill at 1-in-132 past Low House Crossing. This signalbox

Long Meg and Her Daughters

THE STONE circle of Long Meg is a couple of miles to the east of the railway. One of the finest stone circles in the north of England, the circle has a diameter of about 350ft, the second biggest in the country. Long Meg is the tallest of the 69 stones, about 12ft high, with three mysterious symbols, its four corners facing the points of the compass and standing some 60ft outside the circle. The stones probably date from about 1500BC, and it was likely to have been used as a meeting place or for some form of religious ritual. Long Meg is made of local red sandstone, whereas the daughters are boulders of rhyolite, a form of granite. William Wordsworth wrote: "Next to Stonehenge it is beyond dispute the most notable relic that this or probably any other country contains."

Local legend claims that Long Meg was a witch who with her daughters was turned to stone for profaning the Sabbath as they danced wildly on the moor. The circle is supposedly endowed with magic, so that it is impossible to count the same number of stones twice, but if you do then the magic is broken. Surprisingly for such a valuable ancient monument, a road runs right through the circle and visitors park their cars within it.

Long Meg pictured with some of her daughters.

remains open controlling the level crossing and dates back to 1890, but the crossing gates were replaced by lifting barriers in 1975. The line crosses the seven arch Drybeck viaduct before starting to climb again to Armathwaite.

Armathwaite is a pleasant Cumbrian village with the River Eden flowing through it, and renowned for its salmon fishing and superb walks along the river. It contains Armathwaite Castle, a four-storey pele tower, adapted into a country house in 1752 by William Sanderson.

Just south of Armathwaite, beside the river, there are five remarkable carvings of faces in the sandstone cliff.

The original Armathwaite station building, now a private house, is a medium sized style station built from local red sandstone. The waiting shelter on the Up platform is a good example of a stone waiting shelter in traditional Midland style.

Like many stations on the line, Armathwaite was closed between 1970 and 1986. The signalbox closed in 1983, but in 1992 the Friends of the Settle-Carlisle Railway completed their first signalbox restoration. Dating from 1899, the box has been repainted in Midland Railway colours. It remains in its original position. A notable feature of Midland Railway signalboxes is that the four corner timbers of the structure are actually signal posts and taper slightly towards the top.

From Armathwaite, the line drops briefly to the 176 yard Armathwaite viaduct before recommencing the climb through Armathwaite and the two Baron Wood tunnels.

The river can be seen in a deep twisting gorge below to the east. There was once a private siding at Baron Wood, for the Ley family of Lazonby Hall, the owners of the forestry through which the line passes. The timber was used for pit-props during the Second World War and these were transported by rail.

SR unrebuilt Bulleid West Country Pacific No. 34092 *City of Wells* passes Low House signalbox north of Armathwaite on February 13, 1982.

Passing Howe & Co's Sidings signalbox with the Railway Touring Company's 'Waverley' returning from Carlisle to York in August 2012 is LMS 'Black Five' 4-6-0 No. 45305. DAVE COLLIER

SR 4-6-0 No. 850 *Lord Nelson* accelerates away from Carlisle past Howe & Co's sidings with a 'Cumbrian Mountain Pullman' on March 3, 1984. There was once an extensive array of sidings here with short branches to a tile works, plaster works and a brickworks.

Although situated in Lazonby, the station was renamed Lazonby and Kirkoswald in 1895. Like many other stations on the line, it was closed on May 4, 1970, when local passenger services between Skipton & Carlisle were withdrawn. The platforms and buildings survived however, and following several years of use by Dalesrail excursions it was reopened on a full-time basis in July 1986. The station building is in use as offices and the nearby goods shed is also in commercial use.

Having passed through the short tunnel south of Lazonby, the line crosses the River Eden on 137 yard Eden Lacy viaduct, known to the engineers' department as Long Meg viaduct.

Very close by is Long Meg signalbox, built by BR in 1955, which controlled access to the plaster works, which despatched trains mainly to Northwich. The sidings closed in 1975 but the 'box remained open for a further eight years and was retained for occasional use after that. It still stands but in a derelict condition.

Little Salkeld station closed in 1970 but was not reopened in 1986, and is now a private house. Little Salkeld Watermill, built in 1745, is a traditional English 18th century watermill. It is Cumbria's only watermill still in full operation. Its organic bread and all-purpose flours are available in specialist shops throughout the UK. It operated an award-winning organic vegetarian café until this was forced to close during the COVID-19 pandemic of 2020-21.

Lacy's Caves are a series of five chambers in the red sandstone cliff of River Eden, just north of Little Salkeld. They are named after Lieutenant-Colonel Samuel Lacy of Salkeld Hall, who commissioned their carving in the 18th century. The reason for their creation is unknown but they were used by Lacy for entertaining guests and the area was originally planted with ornamental gardens.

Langwathby can be translated as Long (Lang) ford (wath) village (by), referring to the fording

Low House Crossing signalbox.

LNER A3 Pacific No. 4472 *Flying Scotsman* approaches Armathwaite tunnel in April 1980.

The signalbox at Armathwaite, restored by the Friends of the Settle & Carlisle Line.

The gradient post on the Down platform at Armathwaite.

BR Standard 4MT 2-6-4T No. 80080 heads away from Armathwaite on March 4, 1993, with a crew training special.

of the River Eden which runs along the edge of the village. The village is in the Guinness Book of Records as having the country's longest-lasting temporary bridge built back in 1968 and still waiting to be replaced. A party was held to celebrate its 50th anniversary in 2018. The station at Langwathby was closed between 1970 and 1986, the main station buildings are now in use as the Brief Encounter Cafe.

South of the border for the very first time since its purchase for preservation by John Cameron in 1966, LNER A4 Pacific No. 60009 *Union of South Africa* passes Baron Wood on March 31, 1984.

LMS Jubilee 4-6-0 No. 45596 *Bahamas* passes through Baron Wood cutting on August 31, 1990.

LMS Princess Coronation Pacific No. 46229 *Duchess of Hamilton* emerges from Baron Wood tunnel with a 'Cumbrian Mountain Express' on November 5, 1983, carrying a wreath on its smokebox for Remembrance Day.

LNER A3 Pacific No. 4472 *Flying Scotsman* heads north at Baron Wood on May 16, 1992.

It should have been *Duchess of Sutherland*. Having taken over from the stricken No. 46233 on August 11, 2012, West Coast Railways' Class 47 No. 47237 approaches Lazonby over two hours late with a northbound 'Cumbrian Mountain Express'.

A BR special heads north at Lazonby behind 'celebrity' Class 25 D7672 and Class 47 No. 47422 on April 24, 1990.

The station building at Langwathby, a good example of the medium-sized Midland Railway design.

The waiting shelter at Langwathby, on the left of the photograph, was renovated by the Friends of the Settle-Carlisle Railway.

LNER K4 2-6-0 No. 61994 *The Great Marquess* passes Lazonby with the Southbound Statesman Rail 'Fellsman' returning from Carlisle on August 8, 2012.

A Northern Rail service crosses Eden Lacy viaduct.

LNER A3 Pacific No. 4472 *Flying Scotsman* passes Long Meg with an excursion from Carlisle to York on July 4, 1987.

SR Bulleid West Country Pacific No. 34092 *City of Wells* works an early morning Appleby Round Table excursion to York past Little Salkeld on September 26, 1987.

A Down Northern Rail service passes the Midland Hotel as it arrives at Lazonby.

CHAPTER 24

Langwathby-Appleby

AFTER A couple of short downhill sections either side of Lazonby, the line is now climbing most of the way to Appleby, on gradients as steep as 1-in-120, but generally somewhat easier. To the west is the wide expanse of the Eden Valley, but to the east the Pennines are closing in with the line running alongside Cross Fell, the highest mountain in the Pennines.

After passing through the quaintly-named 164 yard Waste Bank tunnel, the line enters the more substantial 661 yard Culgaith tunnel, emerging to pass Culgaith station, this section is the longest section of level track on the line.

Culgaith is first recorded in the reign of Henry I. It was close enough to the Scottish border to be at risk from Scottish raids throughout the Middle Ages. In 1468 villagers shared a watch with neighbouring townships.

Culgaith station was unique. The MR had no intention of building a station at all but the local vicar, the Reverend Atkinson, backed by the villagers, requested one and the MR agreed, but it was not built until 1880 and the expected goods shed never materialised. The station was built in a style totally different to all the others on the line, with mainly wooden platforms and a wooden waiting

The 1908 Midland Railway Culgaith signal box.

shelter on the Down platform. The original signalbox was replaced in 1908 by the present one which remains open, controlling the level crossing.

Beyond Culgaith the line passes under a high bridge, then crosses the 86 yard four arch Crowdundle viaduct and passes New Biggin station. The MR decided to call its station at Newbiggin 'New Biggin' although the place is always spelt as one word. It closed in 1970, but the buildings still stand and are now in private ownership.

Just south of Newbiggin are the gypsum works. British Gypsum absorbed the companies of McGhie's and the Gotham Company Ltd but the railway still referred to it as McGhie's. When gypsum was quar-

LNER A4 Pacific No. 60009 *Union of South Africa* coasts through Culgaith with a northbound 'Cumbrian Mountain Express' on April 20, 1984.

The unique station building at Culgaith. The standard design of Settle & Carlisle line station clocks as supplied by W Potts & Sons of Leeds.

LMS Princess Coronation Pacific No. 46229 *Duchess of Hamilton* emerges from Culgaith tunnel and passes the signalbox and closed station on June 9, 1984.

ried here, the quarries were known as Kirkby Thore and shunted by a Barclay 0-4-0ST. The plant has produced plaster since 1910 and plasterboard since the 1960s.

Now the sidings are where the daily gypsum trains from Drax and other power stations terminate. There are still four local mines – three drift and a quarry – from where gypsum is locally extracted and has been for more than two centuries.

Kirkby Thore British Gypsum sidings are often referred to as Newbiggin, but are actually at Kirkby Thore. However, Kirkby Thore station was on a completely different line, the continuation of the NER Stainmore line through Appleby, joining the WCML at Penrith.

Kirkby Thore village is situated near to the confluence of the rivers Eden and Troutbeck. It got its name from a temple dedicated to the main idol of the pagan Saxons called Thor, the God of thunder, who they worshipped every Thursday – Thor of course gave his name to Thursday. The village is on the site of a Roman cavalry camp called Bravoniacum and Roman coins, tombstones, sandals, urns, earthen vessels and the cusp of a spear have been found in the area. The Maiden Way Roman road leads from Kirkby Thore to Magnis (Carvoran) on Hadrian's Wall.

Long Marton station was built as part of Contract No. 3 for the construction of the line. The line was split into four contracts, No. 3 being from Kirkby Stephen to New Biggin. There were three standard designs for all station buildings on the line, unsurprisingly known as Small, Medium (or Intermediate) and Large.

Long Marton is now the only Intermediate station on Contract No. 3, since the demolition of Crosby Garrett in 1948. It is built of brick as well as stone. Appleby is of similar construction, but is of the Large design.

Against the backdrop of snow-covered Cross Fell, SR 4-6-0 No. 850 *Lord Nelson* approaches Appleby on March 3, 1984.

The station is in private hands but the owner was fortunate enough to be put in touch with Michael Potts, the grandson of the last proprietor of W Potts & Sons of Leeds, the makers of all the Settle-Carlisle clocks, who had a similar clock which could be altered to match the original, and an identical outer face. He bought the clock and had the lettering altered to match the original. It now adorns the station.

Long Marton closed in 1970 and in the early hours of a Sunday morning, British Rail ripped out the platforms, taking the good stone away, and probably dashed any hope of reopening. Long Marton would have been a prime candidate, being one of the biggest villages on the line and it seems that much smaller stations did not have their platforms removed.

Cross Fell is the highest point in the Pennines at 2930ft. It is located at the northern end of the Pennine moors and has extensive views of the Lake District. The east and west coasts, the southern uplands of Scotland and the Cheviots can also be seen from here. The Pennine Way long-distance path goes over Cross Fell from Dufton via Great Dun Fell to Garrigill and Alston.

Snow has been known to lie on Cross Fell for up to 140 days a year, and three of England's major rivers rise near to the summit – the Tyne, the Tees and the Wear.

In times gone by Cross Fell was associated with demons and was often known as the Fiends Fell, possibly because of the great wind it can produce in the valley of the Eden to its west. Known as the Helm Wind, this fierce gale of hurricane proportions, can strike most unexpectedly especially during the spring.

BR Standard 9F 2-10-0 No. 92220 *Evening Star* passes Newbiggin with a southbound 'Cumbrian Mountain Express' on April 23, 1984.

The S&C does not normally look quite as industrialised as this. The Up loaded and Down empty Killoch (Ayrshire) to Ferrybridge coal trains pass at Hale Grange close to the gypsum works.

LNER A3 Pacific No. 60532 *Blue Peter* heads a North Eastern Locomotive Preservation Group railtour towards Appleby on March 6, 1993.

The British Gypsum works at Kirkby Thore.

CHAPTER 25

Appleby

APPLEBY, WHICH occupies a strategic position in the Eden valley, developed as the market and county town of Westmorland after the Norman Conquest, and has a population now of approximately 2500. Its name was simply Appleby, until the sweeping local government changes of 1974, when the local authority changed the town's name to Appleby-in-Westmorland in order to preserve the name of the county which would otherwise have disappeared.

Several neglected estates, castles and churches in the area were restored in the 17th century by Lady Anne Clifford, daughter of the third Earl of Cumberland. She took up residence in Appleby Castle for a while.

Running north from the castle entrance to the cloisters which were designed by Sir Robert Smirke in 1811, Appleby town centre has a remarkably wide main street, Boroughgate, which has been described as one of the finest in England.

Appleby is now well-known for its horse fair which was set up by charter in 1685 as a fair for horse trading. It runs for a week in June, ending on the second Wednesday. The largest of its kind, it has become world famous, attracting a huge gypsy gathering.

Appleby station was known as Appleby West from 1952. Nearby was Appleby East on the NER line from Kirkby Stephen to Penrith on the WCML, which closed in 1962. The buildings of Appleby East still survive, and the connection between the two lines remains and is used as sidings. Appleby West did not revert to plain 'Appleby' until 1968 though.

The NER line remained in use to serve the MoD depot at Warcop and the track remained in situ following closure and is the subject of a preservation scheme known as the Eden Valley Railway which now runs trains on summer weekends over a short distance from Warcop towards Appleby.

Appleby was the only station on the Settle & Carlisle line to have a footbridge and has the longest platforms on the line. The footbridge was not installed until 1901, but quickly collapsed and the present main girder dates from 1902. The building is of the Large design of brick with stone dressing.

The original signalbox was situated on the Down side of the line at the end of the platform and was named Appleby North but was destroyed by fire in 1951. The present box was built by BR on the opposite side of the line and to an LMS design, with a standard pre-1943 LMS lever frame with 20 levers, extended to 25 when Appleby West at the other end of the station closed in 1973.

LMS Princess Royal Pacific No. 46203 *Princess Margaret Rose* accelerates away from Appleby with a southbound 'Cumbrian Mountain Express' on August 20, 1984.

GWR 4-6-0 No. 4979 *Wootton Hall* awaits restoration at the skills and heritage centre alongside the main line at Appleby.

The water tower and water crane at the end of the Up platform were installed by the Appleby Round Table for the use of the numerous steam specials on the line.

LMS Jubilee 4-6-0 No. 5690 *Leander* brings Statesman Rail's 'Fellsman' out of the siding at Appleby on August 17, 2008. Southbound steam specials frequently reverse into the siding to allow a service train to overtake.

MR Compound 4-4-0 No. 1000 and LMS Jubilee 4-6-0 No. 5690 *Leander* perform a photographic runpast for train passengers in snowy conditions at Appleby on February 12, 1983.

LMS Jubilee 4-6-0 No. 5593 *Kolhapur* departs from Appleby northbound on March 21, 1987.

CHAPTER 26

Appleby-Kirkby Stephen

Having departed from Appleby, the line initially drops down to Ormside viaduct, from where the real climb to Ais Gill summit begins. Although the line still follows the valley of the River Eden, it needs to maintain a gradient of 1-in-100 to gain sufficient height, and quickly climbs well above the bottom of the valley.

The small village of Great Ormside was once the seat of the Viking warrior Orm. In the churchyard of St James' Church is an ancient cross socket dated 1643, and here in the early 19th century, the Ormside Bowl was found. This outstanding piece of Saxon metalwork dates from the 9th century, and is now held in a museum in York.

Ormside station was an early closure, in June 1952. The 200 yard 10-arched Ormside viaduct carries the line across the River Eden, from where it is a 1-in-100 climb through Helm tunnel and on to Griseburn viaduct.

Helm Tunnel is 571 yards long and takes the line through Heights Hill. It took three years to build and was completed in 1873. The seven-arch Griseburn viaduct is exactly half way from Carlisle to Settle Junction and the gradient eases briefly to 1-in-166.

Crosby Garrett station was closed in 1952 but the main station building was one of the few on the line to be demolished, four years earlier in 1948. The line then crosses the 110-yard Crosby Garrett viaduct high above the village and then through the 181 yard Crosby Garrett tunnel.

The parish of Crosby Garrett dates back to the 13th century and was formerly called Crosby Garret with just one 't' – and before that Crosby Gerard. In 2011 the parish had a population of 195, estimated at 188 in 2019.

Emerging from Crosby Garrett tunnel, the line curves sharply to the east and crosses Smardale viaduct, the tallest on the line, built entirely of grey limestone, 130ft above Scandal Beck.

The most southerly span of the viaduct crosses the trackbed of the NER's Stainmore line, from Kirkby Stephen to the WCML at Tebay. Local passenger services on this line ceased in 1952 but a summer Saturdays Newcastle-Blackpool holiday train continued to run until the 1960s. Smardale station building on the NER line survives and is in private hands.

The Crosby Garrett Helmet

THE CROSBY Garrett Helmet is a brass Roman cavalry helmet dating from the late first to mid third century AD. It was found by an unnamed metal detectorist near Crosby Garrett in May 2010, close to a Roman road, but some distance from any recorded Roman settlements. The helmet is thought to have been used for ceremonial occasions rather than for combat. Similar helmets found in Britain are the Ribchester Helmet (found in 1796), the Hallaton Helmet (2000) and the Newstead Helmet (1905), though it has closer parallels with helmets found in southern Europe.

Dr Ralph Jackson, senior curator of Romano-British Collections at the British Museum, has described the helmet as "... an immensely interesting and outstandingly important find ... Its face mask is both extremely finely wrought and chillingly striking, but it is as an ensemble that the helmet is so exceptional and, in its specifics, unparalleled. It is a find of the greatest national (and, indeed, international) significance."

On October 7, 2010, the helmet was sold at Christie's for £2.3 million to an undisclosed private buyer. Tullie House Museum and Art Gallery in Carlisle sought to purchase the helmet, with the support of the British Museum but was outbid.

The proceeds of the auction would of course have easily paid for the necessary repairs to Ribblehead viaduct in the 1980s.

SR King Arthur 4-6-0 No. 777 *Sir Lamiel* and LMS 'Black Five' 4-6-0 No. 5407 head south near Stockber on April 3, 1982.

SR 4-6-0 No. 850 *Lord Nelson* emerges from Helm Tunnel and passes Breaks Hall on March 3, 1984. JOHN WHITELEY

LMS 'Black Five' 4-6-0 No. 44932 crosses Crosby Garrett viaduct with the southbound 'Waverley' on September 2, 2012.

Northern Viaduct Trust

SMARDALE GILL viaduct on the NER predates Smardale viaduct, being completed in 1861. The viaduct was designed by Sir Thomas Bouch for the South Durham and Lancashire Union Railway and the construction contracted to Mr Wrigg, costing £11,928 to build.

The bridge, which was built of local stone has 14 arches and is 90ft high and 550ft long. It was single tracked despite being wide enough for a double line. The SDLUR was worked by the Stockton & Darlington Railway and became part of the North Eastern Railway. After the line closed in 1962 the viaduct fell into disrepair, and by the 1980s the structure had become dangerous and was to be demolished. But it became a listed building, and British Rail offered £230,000 (the estimated cost of demolition) towards its restoration.

A charitable trust, the Northern Viaduct Trust was formed in 1989. The cost of repairs was £350,000 which included masonry repair, a new deck and waterproofing, and structural work, completed in 1992. The trust has since carried out restoration work on Podgill and Merrygill viaducts, also on the NER line.

An East Midlands Trains HST crosses the viaduct on a UK Railtours trip from St Pancras on August 18, 2012.

SR unrebuilt Bulleid West Country Pacific No. 34092 *City of Wells* crosses Ormside viaduct on February 13, 1982.

LMS Princess Coronation Pacific No. 46229 *Duchess of Hamilton* heads the 'Cumbrian Mountain Express' past Smardale on November 5, 1983.

BR Standard 4MT 2-6-4T No. 80080 sweeps round the curve at Smardale with a crew-training trip from Carlisle to Kirkby Stephen on March 4, 1993.

Virgin Trains Class 57 No. 57307 heads the diverted 9.03 Euston-Glasgow over Smardale viaduct on June 2, 2007. JOHN WHITELEY

CHAPTER 27

Kirkby Stephen

THE SECOND market town on the southbound run from Carlisle is Kirkby Stephen but this time the railway misses it by a mile and a half. Although still following the Eden Valley, the river flows through the centre of the town but the line has now climbed well above the river and must maintain its height if it is to reach Ais Gill summit without the gradient exceeding the stipulated 1-in-100.

Around the 10th century much of this area was settled by the Danes, often referred to as Vikings, and many places have old Norse names. Kirk-by is said to mean a church-centre. By 1090 the village was recorded as Cherkaby Stephen. This might be an Anglo-Saxon word 'stefan' meaning moor: church centre on the moor, which would account for the local pronunciation of 'Stewen' instead of Stephen.

The sizeable and elegant red sandstone parish church of Kirkby Stephen is often referred to as the 'Cathedral of the Dales'. The original central tower was replaced by the present bell tower on the end after collapsing for a second time in the 16th century.

In the centre of town is a bridge known as Frank's Bridge around which are houses converted from brewery buildings. The bridge is a 17th century corpse lane bridge and the coffins could be rested on stones at one end on their way from nearby villages.

'Frank' is thought to have been Francis Birbeck, who was a brewer. Naturally, there is said to be a ghost which haunts the bridge and can be heard jangling her chains, leading to her being known as Jangling Annas, who is thought to have been a prisoner at Hartley Castle but after escaping, drowned in the river because of the weight of her chains. Opposite was the old R Winters brewery and there were at one time 17 pubs and inns in Kirkby Stephen.

It is an area rich in myths and legends, prehistoric settlements and burial mounds, pele towers,

BR Standard Britannia Pacific No. 70013 *Oliver Cromwell* passes Kirkby Stephen southbound with a Railway Touring Company 'Cumbrian Mountain Express' on March 31, 2012.

medieval halls, Norman castles and Roman forts. Near the villages of Musgrave, Wharton and Waitby, some of the finest Celtic and medieval cultivation terraces in the country can be seen. Kirkby Stephen was granted its market charter in 1353, and became a thriving market town for local agricultural produce. Drover's roads bought livestock for sale and packhorse routes carried goods across the Pennines and down the Eden Valley. The economic history of the area has left a network of public footpaths, bridleways and quiet lanes.

In 1900 Kirkby Stephen station on the Settle & Carlisle was renamed 'Kirkby Stephen and Ravenstonedale' but reverted back to 'Kirkby Stephen' in 1935. Then in 1953 it became 'Kirkby Stephen West' to differentiate it from the former NER station at Kirkby Stephen East. From 1968 though, for the third time the MR station became just 'Kirkby Stephen', but just for two years until closure in 1970.

Kirkby Stephen was the only station on the line to be provided with a first class waiting room by the MR.

Reopened in 1986, the station is now leased by the Settle and Carlisle Railway Trust, which comprehensively restored it in 2005.

The main buildings now incorporate a caretaker's flat, offices and the Midland Room, opened in July 2011, which includes a café and exhibition of items related to the Settle and Carlisle railway. Despite the distance from the town to the station, it was not until 2011 that a properly surfaced path was laid for the use of pedestrians and cyclists.

The MR signalbox at Kirkby Stephen West was replaced by a flatroofed BR 'box in 1974 containing a 20-lever LMS standard frame previously at Kendal. The MR box had always been known as Kirkby Stephen Midland to avoid confusion with Kirkby Stephen West box at Kirkby Stephen East station!

The Stainmore Railway – Kirkby Stephen East

THE FIRST railway to reach the town did build a substantial station convenient for the town. Kirkby Stephen East was built in 1860-61 at the joint expense of the two railway companies which met at this point – the South Durham and Lancashire Union (which ran from Spring Gardens Junction, through Barnard Castle and over the Pennines to Tebay on the West Coast Main Line) and the Eden Valley (which ran from KSE through Appleby to Clifton Junction, south of Penrith, also on the West Coast Main Line).

The engineer for both of these railways was Sir Thomas Bouch, best known for his ill-fated bridge across the Firth of Tay.

In 1862, both railways became part of the Stockton and Darlington Railway and, the following year, the S&D itself became part of the North Eastern Railway. It was never a double track main line railway in the sense of the S&C but a trans-Pennine secondary route carrying heavy coal, limestone and iron ore traffic but using only moderately-sized engines. The railway closed as a through route in 1962, but the branch as far as Hartley quarry remained open for several years, and Kirkby Stephen East station was never demolished.

Today the Stainmore Railway Company has reintroduced steam trains over a short length of reinstated track from Kirkby Stephen East station on summer weekends.

BR Standard 2MT 2-6-0 No. 78019 heads a train out of Kirkby Stephen East station on the Stainmore Railway. MAURICE BURNS

Kirkby Stephen station looking south, complete with new footbridge, installed in 1998 and previously at Guiseley.

A Carlisle-Leeds service arrives at Kirkby Stephen.

The Prince and the Duchess

HRH Prince Charles can be seen on the platform at Kirkby Stephen alongside *Duchess of Sutherland*.

LMS Princess Coronation Pacific No. 6233 *Duchess of Sutherland* departs from Kirkby Stephen with the Royal Train on March 22, 2005.

KIRKBY STEPHEN'S moment of glory came on March 22, 2005, when it was visited by HRH the Prince of Wales, who arrived on the Royal Train, steam hauled from Hellifield by LMS Princess Coronation Pacific No.6233 *Duchess of Sutherland*. Prince Charles unveiled a plaque to commemorate his visit to the recently renovated station, and then joined Carlisle driver John Finlinson, fireman Brian Grierson and inspector Jim Smith on 6233's footplate for the 15 minute run to Appleby.

The first Britannia over the S&C since August 11, 1968, BR Standard Pacific No. 70000 *Britannia* heads south through Kirkby Stephen on September 7, 1991.

CHAPTER 28

Kirkby Stephen-Ais Gill

HEADING SOUTH away from Kirkby Stephen, the outline of Wild Boar Fell is coming closer, marking the summit of the line at Ais Gill. The gradient remains at an unremitting 1-in-100 except for a short section after Birkett tunnel, towards Mallerstang. The 424-yard Birkett tunnel passes through the Pennine Fault.

Mallerstang is the name given to the parish which covers the area from Birkett tunnel to Ais Gill, but there is no settlement with that name. Nevertheless, the MR considered giving Mallerstang a station, but the cost of a long steep access road which the MR was not prepared to finance eventually precluded it being built, although there was a signalbox until 1969.

Outhgill was the birthplace in 1791 of Michael Faraday, who discovered electricity.

The Settle & Carlisle reaches its highest point at Ais Gill summit, 1169ft above sea level. Ais Gill summit is not only the highest but one of the best-known main line railway summits in Britain. Unlike some summits such as Woodhead, Standedge or even the other one on the S&C at Blea Moor, Ais Gill is not in a tunnel, it is right alongside the main road, open and easily accessible, not only a highly scenic location but one where you hardly need to move away from your car to photograph southbound trains on the last few yards to the summit with the sun in the right position all afternoon. Even Shap summit, is behind a cement works, difficult to access and scenically not in the same league as Ais Gill.

Ais Gill is the southernmost of the hamlets that comprise the parish of Mallerstang, situated on the gill itself which flows down from Wild Boar Fell and is crossed by Ais Gill viaduct. Where the Ais Gill joins Hell Gill, they combine to eventually form the River Eden, which the railway has followed all the way from Carlisle.

Ais Gill summit is a mile south of the gill which gives it its name, and the MR built workers' cottages close to the summit, which are known as Ais Gill Cottages. From these cottages, a road crosses the railway virtually at the summit and continues east to cross Hell Gill at Hell Gill Bridge, just half a mile away, and recognised as the watershed of the Pennines. Just half a mile to the south is the infant River Ure which flows south, then east through Wensleydale and on to the North Sea Hell Gill in fact flows right alongside the line at milepost 260 between the two overbridges at Ais Gill. The Midland Railway might have been more geographically correct in calling its summit, signalbox and

The engine is blowing off and the cab storm sheet is flapping in the wind but a tiny patch of sunshine intercepts LNER A2 Pacific No. 60532 *Blue Peter* as it crosses Birkett Common on March 21, 1992. A2 Pacifics had regular duties on the line in the early 1960s but this was the first time No. 60532 had run on the line since its return to main line condition by the North Eastern Locomotive Preservation Group.

LMS 'Black Five' 4-6-0 No. 44932 passes Wharton Dykes just south of Kirkby Stephen with Statesman Rail's 'Fellsman' on August 26, 2012.

One of the most unusual steam trains to have been seen on the Settle & Carlisle; North British Railway J36 0-6-0 No. 673 *Maude* crosses Ais Gill viaduct with two Caledonian coaches on May 17, 1980, en route from Falkirk to Bold colliery for the Rocket 150 celebrations.

Pendragon Castle

CLOSE TO Birkett common are the remains of the 12th century Pendragon Castle. Legend has it that it is here where Uther Pendragon, the father of King Arthur, died. It was abandoned after a raiding Scottish army set fire to it in 1341, but was rebuilt in 1360. It was left in ruins by another fire in 1541 and was restored in the mid-17th century by Lady Anne Clifford... but the castle gradually fell back into ruin after her death.

LNER A3 Pacific No. 4472 *Flying Scotsman* is high above the valley on Mallerstang edge with a private charter train for its then-owner Sir William McAlpine on June 16, 1978.

BR Standard Britannia Pacific No. 70013 *Oliver Cromwell* passes above the settlement of Angerholme on the climb of Mallerstang, with the Railway Touring Company's 'Cumbrian Mountain Express' of March 31, 2012. CRAIG OLIPHANT

For the first time since September 1967 a BR green Jubilee with a train of maroon Mk.1 stock heads south over the S&C, but it nearly didn't look like this. The Bahamas Locomotive Society, owner of No. 45596 *Bahamas*, had hired a support coach from the owner of No. 34092 *City of Wells* and it was green. A fund was started by enthusiasts and photographers to pay for the coach to be repainted to match the rest of the train. *Bahamas* crosses Ais Gill viaduct on August 17, 1990.

cottages Hell Gill, but perhaps its God-fearing directors were a little wary of its connotations.

Ais Gill is dominated by the 2323ft Wild Boar Fell, the fourth highest fell in the Yorkshire Dales or the fifth, if counting the nearby and 3ft higher High Seat. Neither are at present in the national park, although its boundaries could be extended.

The fell gets its name from the wild boar which inhabited the area over 500 years ago, but it is unusual, for this area of Viking settlement, that its old Norse name seems to have disappeared, whereas the names of many of its features, such as The Nab, Dolphinsty etc. retain their Norse origin.

A tusk, claimed to be of "the last wild boar caught on the fell" is kept in Kirkby Stephen parish church.

Up to around the mid-19th century, the Millstone Grit, which forms the flat top of the fell, was used for making millstones, and some partly formed millstones can be seen on the eastern flank of the fell.

There have been three serious railway accidents near Ais Gill. The Hawes Junction crash of 1910 was described earlier, but a further serious incident occurred in 1913.

Two passenger trains left Carlisle for St Pancras in the early hours of September 2, and the locomotives on both trains struggled on the gradients of the S&C. The first train stalled just short of the summit, and the crew made the mistake of telling the guard that they would only be standing for a few

LNER K4 2-6-0 No. 61994 *The Great Marquess* passes milepost 260 (from St Pancras) with Statesman Rail's 'Fellsman' on August 8, 2012.

minutes, so the guard did not follow the regulations to protect his train.

The second train was slightly lighter but the crew was still struggling. The driver actually walked out of the cab on to the outside footplate to carry out some oiling which was no longer necessary, but old habits died hard, and when he returned he had to help his fireman to get an ejector working, by which time they had passed all the red signals at Mallerstang.

Although they did see the stationary train in front of them, they were unable to stop in time. Sixteen passengers from the first train died and many were injured in both trains.

In 1995, an accident occurred at about 6.55pm in heavy rain and darkness on January 31 when a class 156 Sprinter unit was derailed by a landslide and was struck by a similar train travelling in the opposite direction. The train was an Up train which had to turn back at Ribblehead because flooding on the line.

Following the derailment at Ais Gill, the driver and conductor informed Control at Crewe and turned the lights on the front of the unit to red. No further action was taken and although the driver of the next Up train which had already departed from Kirkby Stephen saw the red light he could not stop in time. The conductor of the first train, Stuart Wilson, was fatally injured in the collision.

LNER K4 2-6-0 No. 61994 *The Great Marquess* passes milepost 260 (from St Pancras) with Statesman Rail's 'Fellsman' on August 8, 2012.

A Class 45 Peak tops the summit with an Up Glasgow-Nottingham. The signalbox closed in 1981 and the passing loops were removed. The box is preserved at the Midland Railway Centre at Butterley. The view at this point is now obscured by trees as is sadly the case at many locations on the line now.

The Network Rail track recording HST has just topped the summit northbound on January 28, 2012.

The classic combination in classic Settle & Carlisle weather. MR Compound 4-4-0 No. 1000 and LMS Jubilee 4-6-0 No. 5690 *Leander* top Ais Gill on February 12, 1983.

CHAPTER 29

The Future

It is easy to criticise BR's management in the 1980s for wanting to close the Settle & Carlisle, and the decision in 1989 to reprieve it would appear to be a vindication of that viewpoint. It is also easy to take the view that privatisation has been a disaster for the railway industry, but hindsight is a wonderful thing.

The fact is that the privatisation of the railways has coincided with a tremendous boom in rail travel, especially in the leisure market, which no one could have predicted. Maybe privatisation has not been the single most influential factor in this boom, maybe it would have happened anyway, and maybe the nationalised BR would have reacted just as positively. In fact it would appear that leisure rail travel was on the increase already in the 1980s and circumstances in 1989 were vastly different to those in 1980 when BR first sought to close the line.

The campaign to save it may simply have bought sufficient time for it to be seen that the line could have a future as traffic increased significantly even when those in authority were doing everything they could to discourage it. In fact, the closure plans clearly provided a major impetus to encourage traffic growth.

Back in the 1960s, like all railways, the S&C was a public service, heavily subsidised, and would never generate sufficient passenger traffic to justify its retention once car ownership started to become the norm. The 1970s was a decade of recession, industrial unrest and uncertainty. BR was under pressure from successive governments to continue to modernise, to cut costs and close down uneconomic services.

There was enough freight traffic remaining in the 1970s though that closure would have put too much pressure on the east and west coast routes just at the time they needed to go through the modernisation process. The concentration of traditional wagonload freight traffic on to the line kept it going for a few years after the WCML was electrified to Glasgow in 1974, but once this traffic evaporated, the writing really did seem to be on the wall.

It would even seem now that BR management was under political pressure to close the line but was so opposed to such a course of action, it deliberately appointed a manager who would do the exact opposite of what he was appointed to do.

During the Beeching railway closures of the 1960s, every time there was a line closure there was public outrage, but the trains continued to be empty

LMS Princess Coronation Pacific No. 46229 *Duchess of Hamilton* storms past Horton in Ribblesdale with a 'Cumbrian Mountain Express' on October 23, 1983. One day we could see the same engine in its original streamlined form tackling the 'long drag'.

until the very end when everyone wanted to travel on the last train. By the late 1980s it was different.

One of the keys to the line's success over the last three decades is that the British public no longer just take two weeks' holiday per year and spend it on the beach. Days and weekends away throughout the year are now the norm and inland tourist hotspots which would have seen a couple of dozen people on a hot bank holiday in 1963 now see thousands even on winter weekends or midweek throughout the year.

We now have the line, saved and thriving, stations have been reopened and restored and the track has largely been renewed. There was a serious setback in February 2016 when a massive 500,000 ton landslide resulted in the Carlisle to Settle line being closed for over a year – but following the construction of a steel tunnel-line structure to sit beneath the railway it has remained open. Repair work cost a total of £23m.

Today the S&C still uses traditional signalboxes and signalling with a few additional remote-controlled signals but one of the major changes which we will see will be the wholesale abolition of the traditional signalling system.

There are some teething problems with the European Rail Traffic Management System (ERTMS), not least of which is the impracticality of fitting it to British steam engines, but it is coming. When it does, the whole of Network Rail will be controlled by a handful of signalboxes; within a few years, no longer will the traditional signalman be ringing bells and pulling levers in a wooden structure built by the Midland Railway in the 19th century.

Network Rail announced that it was considering a trial of the ERTMS on the Wherry Lines from Norwich to Lowestoft and Great Yarmouth in East Anglia and this new signalling was introduced in February 2020.

Passenger traffic on the S&C would appear to be stable and buoyant – at least it was before COVID-19, which at the time of writing had introduced new uncertainties. Freight traffic though is a different matter. The gypsum traffic was lost to rail and has only returned as it now flows in the opposite direction, the result of environmental pressures on coal-fired power stations.

These power stations were under threat from gas-fired stations, but Russian gas has now become scarce, reviving the fortunes of the coal-fired stations, if only temporarily, and boosting the flow of coal trains over the S&C. There are huge reserves of gas and oil beneath Britain though and once this can be accessed, it will serve Britain's energy needs for another 30 years.

Coal-fired power stations are under increasing threat – with the government attempting to hit a target of banning all coal-fired electricity in the UK by 2025.

Maybe increased speeds and frequency of passenger trains on the West Coast Main Line will see more traffic such as container trains travelling via Blea Moor rather than Shap in the future. The line's future would appear to be far more secure now than at any time in the past 60 years and one day, who knows, it could even be electrified. The S&C is a living railway and must develop in line with the rest of the railway system. It cannot just stand still or look back. The past can be preserved to complement the present, but we should appreciate what we have now and not take it for granted

Index